Sardinia Iconic T Guide 2024

Unique Exploration of Costa Smeralda, Unforgettable Beaches and Natural beauty, Hidden Treasure, Insider Tips, Gastronomic Adventures & Accommodation

Tara D. Hayes

Copyright © 2024 by Tara D. Hayes

All rights reserved. No part of this publication may be reproduced, distributed, or transmitted in any form or by any means, including photocopying, recording, or other electronic or mechanical methods, without the prior written permission of the publisher, except for brief quotations in critical reviews and certain other noncommercial uses permitted by copyright law.

This book is a non-fiction work. All characters, incidents, and dialogue are based on the author's personal experiences, interviews, and research. Any resemblance to actual persons, living or dead, or events is purely coincidental.

While every effort has been made to provide accurate and up-to-date information, neither the author nor the publisher can be held liable for any errors or omissions or for any consequences resulting from the use of this information.

Table of Contents

Part 1: Plan Your Sardinian Escape 6

Chapter 1: Introduction to Sardinia—Unveiling the Mediterranean Jewel 7

    1.1 Brief History of Sardinia 10

    1.2 Geographical and Landscape Highlights 12

    1.3 Why Sardinia? Reasons to visit...................................14

Chapter 2: Essential Travel Planning Information 17

    2.1 When to Visit Sardinia (Based on Weather, Seasons, and Events)..17

    2.2 Visa and Entry Requirements. 20

    2.3 How to Get There: Flights, Ferries, and Other Transportation Options 23

    2.4 Traveling Around Sardinia: Public Transportation, Car Rentals, and Taxis 26

Chapter 3: Understanding Sardinia. 31

    3.1 Currency and Exchange Rates. 31

    3.2 Language and Basic Phrases. 33

    3.2 Local Customs and Etiquette 36

    3.3 Tips and Bargaining...39

    3.4 Health and Safety Information 42

    3.5 Packing Essentials for Your Trip................................45

Part 2: Exploring Sardinia by Region 49

Chapter 4: Breathtaking Coasts 50
  4.1 Costa Smeralda: Luxury, Beaches, and Glamor 50
    4.1.1 Must-see Beaches in Costa Smeralda 50
    4.1.2 Towns and Villages To Explore 54
    4.1.3 Activities and Daytrips 59
  4.2 The Rugged North: Alghero, Stintino, and the Asinara Islands 63
    4.2.1 Stunning Beaches and Natural Beauty 63
    4.2.2 Exploring Historic Alghero. 69
  4.3 Scenic East Coast: Ogliastra and the Baunei Mountains. 77
    4.3.1: Dramatic Landscapes and Hidden Coves 77
    4.3.2 Hiking and Outdoor Activities. 82
  4.4 Southern Shores: Cagliari and Chia 87
    4.4.1 Exploring the Vibrant Capital City, Cagliari. 87
    4.4.2 Relaxing on Chia's Beautiful Beaches. 94
    4.4.3 Archaeological sites and historical gems 99

Part 3: Experience Sardinia 105

Chapter 5, Beaches and Water Activities 106
  5.1 Snorkelling, Diving, and Water Sports Activities 106
  5.2 Boat Tours and Sail Trips 110

Chapter 6: Exploring History and Culture. 116
  6.1 Nuragic Culture and Archaeological Sites 116
  6.2 Phoenician and Roman influences 120

6.3 Folklore, Traditions and Festivals 123

Chapter 7: A Taste of Sardinia... 128

    7.1 Sardinian Cuisine: Local Specialties and Must-Try Recipes 128

    7.2 Wine regions and Sardinian wines 132

    7.3 Restaurants and Nightlife 134

Part 4: Practical Information. 138

Chapter 8: Accommodation Options in Sardinia 139

    8.1 Luxury Hotels and Resorts. 139

    8.2 Boutique Hotels and Charming Bed & Breakfasts 143

    8.3 Self-catering Apartments and Villas 146

    8.4 Camping and glamping sites 149

Chapter 9: Maintaining Connection and Communication .. 152

    9.1 Mobile Phone Coverage and Internet Access 152

    9.2 Staying Safe: Emergency Numbers and Services. 154

Appendix 158

    A1: Maps of Sardinia 158

    A2. Glossary of Sardinian Terms 159

Part 1: Plan Your Sardinian Escape

Chapter 1: Introduction to Sardinia—Unveiling the Mediterranean Jewel

Sardinia, a beautiful island basking in the warm rays of the Mediterranean sun, awaits your exploration. This lovely hideaway offers a one-of-a-kind combination of natural beauty, rich history, and dynamic culture, making it an outstanding holiday destination.

A Look into Sardinia's Past

As you explore Sardinia's history, you will discover a magnificent tapestry weaved by many civilizations. The island has a particularly fascinating chapter with the Nuragic people, a Bronze Age culture that left behind strange stone towers known as Nuraghi. These fantastic monuments, strewn around the island, serve as quiet sentinels, telling stories from a bygone period.
Sardinia's narrative continues with the Phoenicians, Carthaginians, and Romans, each of whom left their imprint. The island then passed under Byzantine and Pisan sovereignty, each time contributing to its cultural wealth.

A Landscape Unlike Any Other.

Prepare to be fascinated by Sardinia's varied scenery. The island's greatest treasure is undeniably its shoreline. Pristine white-sand beaches bordered by turquoise seas invite leisure, while rocky cliffs and secret coves provide a feeling of adventure.
Travel inland to encounter a world of undulating hills, verdant valleys, and spectacular mountain ranges. Hike through unspoiled nature or discover little settlements tucked in stunning surroundings.

Reasons to Fall in Love With Sardinia

Here are some reasons why Sardinia should be your next vacation destination:

Beach Bliss: Whether you want to sunbathe on smooth sand or snorkel in crystal-clear seas, Sardinia's coastline accommodates any beach bum's desires.
Historical Highlights:
- Visit old Nuragic towers.
- Explore Roman remains.
- Immerse yourself in the quaint atmosphere of medieval cities.

Foodie Paradise: Sardinia's unique cuisine highlights fresh, local products. Savor delectable seafood delicacies, delight in handcrafted cheeses, and drink world-class wines.

Hike through stunning landscapes, kayak along the gorgeous shoreline, or explore secret caverns. Sardinia provides a paradise for outdoor lovers.

Cultural Tapestry: Immerse yourself in the colorful culture by attending traditional festivals, listening to evocative folk music melodies, and being enchanted by the Sardinian people's welcoming hospitality.

Begin Planning Your Sardinian Escape.

Sardinia is a location that promises to make a lasting impression on your soul. This first chapter has hopefully whetted your appetite for this Mediterranean treasure. The following parts of this travel guide will provide all the information you need to organize your perfect Sardinian journey. So, pack your luggage, embrace the spirit of discovery, and prepare to discover the wonder of Sardinia!

1.1 Brief History of Sardinia

Sardinia's compelling tale spans millennia, establishing the island's distinct character. As you explore its nooks and crannies, you'll come across vestiges of numerous civilizations, each contributing a brushstroke to the rich tapestry of Sardinian history.

The Nuragic Civilization: A Mysterious Beginning (1800 BC–238 BC)

Your trip through time begins with the Nuragic people, a Bronze Age culture steeped in mystery. They erected the renowned Nuraghi, remarkable beehive-shaped stone structures dispersed around the island. Archaeologists continue to be fascinated by these impressive constructions, some of which are several stories high. Their specific function is unknown; however, they acted as strongholds, halls of worship, or possibly shared housing.

From Phoenicians to Romans: A melting pot of influences.

Phoenician merchants came to Sardinia about the eighth century BC, enticed by the island's abundant resources. They built towns along the coastline, laying the groundwork for future trading routes. The Carthaginians, another powerful maritime force, seized control in the sixth century BC, significantly altering the island's culture and language.

The inevitable battle of empires resulted in Roman domination in the third century BC. The Romans put their stamp on infrastructure by developing roads, aqueducts, and towns. Latin became the primary language, although Phoenician and Carthaginian influences may still be seen in Sardinian place names and rituals.

Medieval Mosaic: From Byzantine to Spanish Rule

Following the collapse of the Roman Empire, Sardinia experienced a period of turmoil. Barbarian invasions undermined Byzantine control, resulting in a fractured political environment. In the 11th century, Pisa, a solid Italian naval republic, took control of most of the island. Their influence may be observed in the architectural style of many Sardinian churches.

By the fourteenth century, the Spanish Crown of Aragon had taken control, ushering in centuries of Spanish dominance. The Kingdom of Sardinia was established during this century when art, architecture, and language flourished. The Spanish language has imprinted on Sardinian dialects, and the cultural impact is seen in festivals and rituals.

Today, Sardinia is an autonomous region with a rich heritage.

Sardinia formally joined a united Italy in 1861. Today, it has a high degree of autonomy, allowing it to maintain its cultural character. Sardinia has traces of all the civilizations that have inhabited the island, including language, gastronomy, architecture, and customs. Explore secluded coves, meander through old ruins, or sample a traditional meal to immerse yourself in Sardinia's rich past.

1.2 Geographical and Landscape Highlights

Sardinia, Italy's second-largest island, has a landscape as varied as its history. Bathed in the warm Mediterranean sun, the island combines stunning coasts, craggy mountain ranges, and undulating hills to create a compelling landscape. This diversity assures that there is something for everyone, from beach bums looking for leisure to explorers looking for new experiences.

Island Paradise: A Mediterranean Gem.

Sardinia is shaped like a gigantic footprint with over 1,800 kilometers of magnificent coastline. The island's western and northern coastlines are characterized by stunning limestone cliffs carved by wind and water. The landmark Capo Caccia provides stunning vistas, and the Costa Verde (Green Coast) is a sight. Hidden coves with crystal-clear waters demand exploration, while quiet beaches offer respites to relaxation.

A feast for the eyes, from dramatic cliffs to pristine beaches.

The eastern and southern coasts provide a distinct scenery. The beautiful Costa Smeralda (Emerald Coast) is known for its opulent resorts and picturesque coves with turquoise seas. The Ogliastra area offers a more isolated and unspoiled beach experience. At the same time, the southern coast includes large expanses of golden sand, with popular spots such as Chia drawing sunbathers and water sports lovers.

Beyond the coast: Mountains, valleys, and rolling hills

Travel inland to see a world of stunning mountain ranges and undulating hills. The island's tallest mountain range, the Gennargentu, provides a playground for hikers with picturesque routes, flowing waterfalls, and stunning panoramic vistas. Much of the central area is covered in rolling hills and lush valleys, punctuated with attractive towns, wineries, and chances to learn about authentic Sardinian culture.

Natural wonders await discovery.

Sardinia's beauty goes beyond the beaches and mountains. The breathtaking Gorroppu Gorge, Europe's deepest canyon, is a must-see for nature lovers. Hidden caverns with stalactites and stalagmites provide a look into the island's underground treasures. Adventurers may visit the Asinara National Park, a protected island refuge renowned for its rich species and pristine ecosystems.

Sardinia's different landscapes, from the spectacular cliffs in the north to the long sandy beaches in the south, provide tourists with many experiences. Whether you want leisure on gorgeous beaches, adventure in the mountains, or exploring lovely towns, this intriguing island will leave an indelible impression.

1.3 Why Sardinia? Reasons to visit

Sardinia, tucked amid the Mediterranean Sea, entices tourists with the promise of memorable adventures. This intriguing island goes beyond the conventional beach vacation, providing a distinct combination of natural beauty, historical history, and lively culture. Here are some reasons why Sardinia should be your next vacation destination:

Beach Bliss: Sardinia's coastline is, without a doubt, its crown treasure. Cala Brandinchi and Cala Cipolla have pristine white sand beaches with turquoise seas lapping at the coast, making them excellent for sunbathing and swimming. Dramatic coves such as Cala Goloritze and Cala Luna, reachable by boat or picturesque trek, provide a feeling of adventure and solitude.

A Journey Through Time: Sardinia's exciting past is reflected in its archeological treasures. Wander among the Nuragic towers and fascinating stone buildings dating back to the Bronze Age, and reflect on the life of the ancient culture that constructed them. Explore Roman remains, attractive medieval towns like Alghero, which has Catalan influences, and spectacular strongholds that tell stories of bygone ages.

A Foodie Paradise: Sardinian food celebrates fresh, local ingredients and traditional recipes handed down through generations. Savor delicious seafood delicacies such as sea urchin spaghetti and fregola alle vongole. Enjoy local cheeses like Pecorino Sardo and wonderful breads like pane carasau, a thin, crispy flatbread. Take advantage of the chance to sample world-renowned Sardinian wines, ranging from the full-bodied Cannonau to the crisp Vermentino.

Adventure awaits: Sardinia is a paradise for outdoor lovers. Hike through the magnificent Gennargentu highlands, past flowing waterfalls, and panoramic views. Kayak around the picturesque coastline to find secret coves and isolated beaches. Explore the breathtaking

Gorroppu Gorge, Europe's deepest canyon, or go spelunking into secret caverns studded with stalactites and stalagmites.

Cultural Tapestry: Immerse yourself in Sardinia's colorful culture. Experience classic festivities such as the Sa Sartiglia jousting contest in Oristano, or be fascinated by beautiful melodies of folk music performed on instruments like the launeddas (triple pipes). Experience the warm hospitality of the Sardinian people, who are noted for their strong attachment to their past and traditions.

Beyond the Tourist Trail: Sardinia provides an opportunity to escape the masses and see a more authentic side of Italy. Explore lovely communities set among rolling hills, where time seems to pause. Visit local markets full of fresh vegetables and homemade crafts. Interact with artisans who preserve ancient crafts, such as weaving and woodcarving.

Sardinia has something for everyone, whether they want to relax on magnificent beaches, learn about its rich history, or immerse themselves in a dynamic culture. This enchanting island provides a fantastic retreat, leaving you eager to return and uncover its hidden gems.

Chapter 2: Essential Travel Planning Information

2.1 When to Visit Sardinia (Based on Weather, Seasons, and Events)

Sardinia's breathtaking beauty may be experienced all year, but the best time to visit depends on what you want from your island retreat. Let's look at the benefits and drawbacks of each season to help you pick when Sardinia will fascinate you most.

Soak Up the Sun: Summer Bliss (June–August)

- **Weather:** Bright sunlight with highs in the mid-30s°C (upper 80s°F) and crystal-clear water. Ideal for beachgoers and watersports lovers.
- **Pros:** Long days, a lively environment, all beaches and activities open, perfect for swimming and tanning.
- **Cons:** Peak tourist season, higher-cost flights and accommodations, and crowded beaches, particularly in famous destinations.

Shoulder Seasons: Golden Opportunities (April-May, September-October)

- **Weather:** Pleasant weather with highs in the mid-20s°C (70s°F), ideal for touring beaches and inland locations. Less rain than in winter.
- **Pros:** Fewer people, cheaper flights and accommodations, and pleasant sightseeing and outdoor sports weather.
- **Cons:** Some beach amenities and water sports alternatives may have restricted hours during the high season.

Escape the Crowds: Winter Tranquility (November to March)

- **Weather:** Cooler temps with periodic rain; specific beaches may be unsuitable for swimming.
- **Pros:** Low visitor numbers, the opportunity to see true village life, and spectacular wildflower displays in the spring.
- The cons: Many restaurants and businesses shut during this time, and outdoor activities may be restricted due to the weather.

Are you a festival fan? Plan your trip around these events:

January: Attend the colorful Sant'Antonio Abate festival in Mamoiada, which includes masked figures and bonfires.

February: Take part in the island's pre-Lenten Carnival events, which include colorful costumes, parades, and live music.

Spring and summer: Many towns and villages conduct traditional Sardinian cultural events, such as the Sardinian Jousting Tournament (Sa Sartiglia) in Oristano.

September: Celebrate the grape harvest with local events such as Barbagia's Grape Festival.

Here's a simple guide to help you find the ideal Sardinian escape:

For assured weather and beach bliss: June to August (be prepared for crowds and increased rates).

For pleasant weather, fewer people, and fantastic deals, April-May or September-October

For an authentic local experience and budget-friendly trip, November to March (be prepared for colder temperatures and restricted amenities).

For cultural immersion, organize your vacation around a particular event.

No matter when you travel, Sardinia's enchantment greets you. So pack your bags, embrace the spirit of discovery, and prepare to find the ideal season for your incredible Sardinian journey!

2.2 Visa and Entry Requirements.

Sardinia, a beautiful island treasure in the Mediterranean, warmly welcomes travelers. However, to guarantee a smooth admission procedure, you must first learn the visa and entry criteria before going on your Sardinian excursion.

Sardinia and Schengen Zone

Sardinia is part of Italy and a member of the Schengen Area, a group of 26 European nations that have removed most internal border restrictions. This implies that if you are a citizen of a Schengen member nation or have a valid Schengen visa, you may visit Sardinia for up to 90 days during 180 days.

Visa-free entry for many nationalities.

The good news for tourists from many countries is that Sardinia, a member of the Schengen Area, permits visa-free access for stays of up to 90 days. This includes nationals of the United States, Canada, Australia, New Zealand, Japan, and most European nations.

Double-check your passport's validity.

Ensure your passport is valid for at least three months after your desired departure date from Sardinia. Some countries may need a longer validity term; therefore, contact the closest Italian embassy or consulate in your native country for the most recent information.

What You Might Need to Show at Immigration:

While a valid passport is required, immigration officers may request extra papers to confirm your reason for the trip and intended stay. Here's what you may need to have easily accessible:

- **Return or onward flight ticket:** This confirms that you intend to depart Sardinia within the visa-free period.

- **Proof of accommodation:** A hotel reservation confirmation or rental agreement demonstrating your intended stay.

- **Proof of adequate funds:** While there is no minimum amount, immigration authorities may want proof that you have enough money to support your stay in Sardinia. This might include bank statements, credit cards, and traveler's checks.

Are you traveling for an extended period or with a different passport?

If you want to remain in Sardinia for more than 90 days or are not a citizen of a visa-free country, you must apply for a Schengen visa at the Italian embassy or consulate in your country. Different visa classes are designed for specific objectives, such as long-term visits, employment, or education. Contact the Italian embassy or consulate for further information on the application procedure and needed paperwork.

Staying informed is the key to a smooth entry.

Visa and entrance restrictions might vary, so it's critical to keep current. The official website of the Italian Ministry of Foreign Affairs *(https://vistoperitalia.esteri.it/home/en)* gives up-to-date information on visa requirements for various nations. Consult the website of the closest Italian embassy or consulate in your native country for further information and application requirements.

By familiarizing yourself with the visa and entrance formalities, you may ensure a smooth and stress-free arrival in Sardinia, enabling you to concentrate on having great experiences on this beautiful island.

2.3 How to Get There: Flights, Ferries, and Other Transportation Options

Sardinia beckons, and getting to this intriguing island paradise is simpler than you think. Several transportation alternatives suit different budgets and travel preferences, assuring a smooth and pleasant trip to begin your Sardinian experience.

Take Flight: Soaring into Sardinia

For a quick and pleasant trip, try flying straight into one of Sardinia's three major airports:

Cagliari Elmas Airport (CAG) is the island's busiest airport, serving major European cities. Depending on the season and airline, prices might vary from low-cost choices like Ryanair and easyJet to more expensive connections.

Olbia Costa Smeralda Airport (OLB): Located in northern Sardinia's famous Costa Smeralda area, this airport handles both scheduled and charter flights. Prices vary according to airline and season; however, they are usually more expensive than at Cagliari Elmas Airport.

Alghero Fertilia Airport (AHO) serves the northwestern coast of Sardinia and provides connections to various European locations. Flight fares might vary depending on the season and airline, although they often fall within the same range as Cagliari Elmas Airport.

Tips for Savvy Flyers:

- Book your flights in advance, particularly during the high season (June-August), to get the best discounts.
- If your destination is the island's north, consider flying into a smaller airport, such as Alghero.
- Explore cheap airlines and compare costs from various carriers to discover the best cost-effective alternative.

Taking the Ferry: A Scenic Journey to Sardinia

Take a boat to Sardinia for a more relaxing and picturesque excursion. Several ferry companies offer routes from mainland Italy, enabling you to bring your vehicle or motorcycle to explore the island on your schedule. Here are some of the major ferry operators:

Grandi Navi Veloci (GNV): This significant ferry operator connects different Italian ports, including Civitavecchia, Genoa, and Livorno, to Sardinia. Ferry fares vary by route, trip time, and cabin type (deck passage or cabin with bed). Expect to pay a premium for speedier routes and accommodations.

Tirrenia: Another well-known ferry operator, Tirrenia, links Sardinia to mainland Italy via ports such as Civitavecchia, Genoa, and Naples. Prices are typically close to GNV, with variances depending on the route and cabin type.

Moby Lines: This ferry business connects mainland Italy, notably Civitavecchia, Livorno, and Piombino, to Sardinia. Prices are competitive, and Moby Lines is renowned for regular specials.

Tips for Ferry Travelers:

- Book your ferry tickets well in advance to prevent sold-out crossings, particularly during peak season.
- Consider the trip time when selecting a ferry route. Direct routes are quicker but more expensive, while indirect routes with stopovers might be more cost-effective.
- Determine if you need a cabin for a pleasant overnight voyage or whether a deck passage is enough for a shorter daylight crossing.

Beyond flights and ferries: Additional Transportation Options

Once you arrive in Sardinia, you have many transportation alternatives to tour the island at your own pace:

- **Rail:** Sardinia's small rail network links several of its main towns and cities. While not the most comprehensive network, it may be a handy and cost-effective choice for short trips.

- **Buses:** A more extensive public bus network connects Sardinia's cities, villages, and seaside resorts. Buses are a fantastic way to explore smaller towns and navigate regions not served by railroads.
- **Car Rentals:** Renting a car provides the greatest freedom to experience Sardinia's landscapes and hidden treasures. Many automobile rental firms operate at airports and large cities. Consider automobile size, fuel economy, and insurance coverage while deciding.

Choosing Your Ideal Gateway

The best way to go to Sardinia depends on your budget, travel style, and destination. Consider flying if you want to arrive quickly. If you want a picturesque ride and the flexibility to transport your automobile, choose a Boat. Once on the island, consider the numerous transportation alternatives to plan the proper schedule for your excellent Sardinian adventure.

2.4 Traveling Around Sardinia: Public Transportation, Car Rentals, and Taxis

Sardinia's fascinating beauty extends beyond its breathtaking coastline. To appreciate the island's appeal, you must journey through lovely towns, majestic mountains, and secluded coves. This book delves into the numerous transportation alternatives available, allowing you to plan the ideal schedule for your Sardinian vacation.

Public transportation is a budget-friendly option.

Although not the most comprehensive in Europe, Sardinia's public transportation network is a handy and cost-effective method to tour the island, particularly for those visiting on a tight budget. Here's an overview of the major options:

Trains: Trenitalia has a modest rail network linking significant towns and cities, including ***Cagliari, Sassari, Olbia, and Porto Torre.*** While train travel may not be the quickest choice, it is a picturesque and pleasant method to travel great distances. Ticket costs vary by route and travel class (standard or comfort).

Buses: ***ARST (Azienda Regionale Sarda Trasporto)*** operates Sardinia's most extensive public transportation network. Buses link cities, villages, and seaside resorts around the island, enabling you to visit places not served by railroads. Tickets may be bought at newsstands, dedicated ARST sales sites, or directly on the bus (a little higher price). Expect to spend a few euros for shorter trips and a little more for longer ones.

Tips For Using Public Transportation:

- Download the ARST mobile app (available for iOS and Android) to browse timetables, buy tickets, and plan your trip ahead of time.
- Buses operate less often in rural regions and may have reduced timetables on weekends and public holidays. Plan appropriately.
- To avoid penalties, validate your ticket when boarding the bus.

Car rentals provide freedom and flexibility.

Consider hiring a vehicle for maximum flexibility and the freedom to see Sardinia's hidden beauties at your speed. Car rental firms are available at airports (Cagliari Elmas, Olbia Costa Smeralda, Alghero Fertilia) and essential cities like Alghero, Cagliari, and Olbia.

- **Costs:** Rental vehicle rates vary based on the season, car size, and insurance coverage. Expect to spend extra during peak season (June-August) for bigger cars with full insurance. Budget-friendly solutions are available, particularly during the shoulder seasons (April-May and September-October), but research costs and inclusions before booking.

- Consider extra expenditures like gasoline, tolls (minor on certain roads), and parking, particularly in central tourist locations. An International

Driving Permit (IDP) is suggested but optional to prevent problems with rental businesses.

Taxis are a convenient but more expensive option.

Taxis are easily accessible at Sardinia's airports, main rail stations, and town centers. They are a handy method to travel, particularly for short distances or late-night trips. However, be warned that taxis are often the most costly mode of transportation on the island.

- **Costs:** Metered fares and beginning costs apply. Taxis cost extra at night, on Sundays, and on public holidays. Before you leave, agree on a fee with the driver, particularly if you need to figure out where you're going.

Choosing Your Ideal Mode of Transportation.

The best method to get about Sardinia depends on your travel preferences and budget. Public transportation is a handy and cost-effective choice for budget-conscious tourists, particularly for seeing large cities and villages served by the rail network. Automobile rentals are the way to go if you want the flexibility to explore secret coves and secluded locations. Taxis are a practical but more expensive choice for short-distance or late-night transport.

By carefully assessing your requirements and interests, you may choose the most appropriate mode of transportation to traverse Sardinia and discover the island's hidden gems.

Chapter 3: Understanding Sardinia.

3.1 Currency and Exchange Rates.

Sardinia, a beautiful Mediterranean island, uses the Euro (EUR) as its official currency. This makes things easier for tourists from most European nations, who will not need to convert their cash upon arrival.

Traveling from outside the Eurozone?

If you're visiting Sardinia from a nation with a foreign currency, bear the following in mind:

Currency conversion rates vary, so checking the current rate before traveling is best. Online tools such as Google Finance and XE Currency Converter may give up-to-date data.

Exchanging currencies: There are many ways to convert your currencies to euros. You may do this at your home bank before leaving, albeit the rates may be less competitive. Exchange offices (cambio) in airports, rail stations, and tourist destinations also provide currency exchange. However, their rates and fees differ. Consider utilizing Sardinia's ATMs (bancomat) to withdraw Euros using your debit or credit card. This is frequently the most convenient and cost-effective choice; however, your bank may charge foreign transaction costs.

Tips for Managing Money in Sardinia:

Carry a mix of cash and credit cards: While credit cards are generally accepted in main tourist destinations, restaurants, and stores, it's always a good idea to have some money on hand for minor purchases, taxis, or unforeseen circumstances. ATMs are widely distributed across Sardinia's villages and cities.

Inform Your Bank: Before your travel, inform your bank that you will use your debit or credit card overseas to prevent any possible account bans due to suspicious behavior.

Beware of Hidden costs: Check your debit or credit card for any expenses related to overseas transactions before depending only on ATMs for cash withdrawals.

General cost considerations in Sardinia:

- **Budget:** Prices vary based on your trip style. Budget for lodging, meals, transportation, attraction admission costs, and any activities you want.
- **Seasonality:** Prices are often higher during peak season (June-August) than during shoulder seasons (April-May and September-October) and off-season (November-March).

- **Location:** Popular tourist places may have higher prices than smaller towns and villages.

Planning your budget ahead of time, keeping currency rates and other costs in mind, can enable a pleasant and financially stress-free discovery of Sardinia's stunning beauty.

3.2 Language and Basic Phrases.

Sardinia has a complex linguistic tapestry. While Italian is the official language, the island also has its distinct language, Sardinian, which many people speak. However, do not worry! Here's a how-to guide for communicating in Sardinia, guaranteeing a seamless and happy encounter.

Italian: The Lingua Franca

Italian is widely spoken and understood across Sardinia. Therefore, it is the preferred language for interacting with people, particularly in tourist regions. You can communicate with merchants, restaurant personnel, and other tourists if you know a few essential Italian words.

Sardinian: A Cultural Gem.

Sardinian is a fascinating language with a rich history, and learning it adds another dimension to your Sardinian experience. While you may only become proficient after some time, knowing a few simple Sardinian words shows respect for the local culture and may go a long way toward winning the people's hearts.

Basic Phrases to Get By:

Here are some critical Italian and Sardinian words to get you started on your Sardinian trip.

Greetings:

- Italian: Ciao (Hello), Buongiorno (Good Morning), Buonasera (Good Evening).
- Sardinian: Bongiorno (Good morning/day); Buonasera (Good evening).

Essential questions:

- **Italian:** Mi scusi (excuse me), per favore (please), Grazie (thank you), prego (you are welcome).
- Sardinian: Iscusa, Per favore, Gràtzias, and Prego.

Useful phrases:

- **Italian:** May I have the account, please? (May I get the bill, please?) Quanto costa? (How much is it?), Non capisco (I don't understand)
- **Sardinian:** Could you please provide me with your account information? (May I get the bill, please?), Cantu Custa? (How much is it?), Non capisco (I don't understand)

Tips For Effective Communication:

- **Speak Slowly and Clear:** Enunciate clearly, mainly while speaking Italian, since some Sardinians may have a little regional accent.
- **Gestures Can Help:** Be bold and utilize hand gestures to enhance your speech. Italians and Sardinians are renowned for their expressive body language.
- A welcoming grin may help cross any language barrier and convey your eagerness to interact.
- Carry a Phrasebook: A compact Italian or Sardinian phrasebook may be helpful, particularly when exploring outside the main tourist destinations.
- Download a Translation App: Several translation applications are available to assist you in translating simple words and signs.

Beyond the basics:

While these fundamental phrases will get you by, knowing more words or phrases about your hobbies (food, tourism, or specialized activities) might improve your experience. Locals appreciate any attempt to speak their language, even if it is just a few words.

Adopting the language and attempting to converse will strengthen your bond with the island and its inhabitants. So, have a lovely travel and a great stay in Sardinia!

3.2 Local Customs and Etiquette

With its magnificent scenery and rich cultural legacy, Sardinia entices those seeking a genuine Italian experience. However, navigating a new culture entails more than just organizing plans. Understanding local traditions and etiquette allows for a seamless and courteous connection with the Sardinian people. Here's a guide to help you enjoy the island's splendor while honoring local customs.

Greetings and interactions:

Warm welcomes: Sardinians are famed for their hospitality. A handshake and a genuine "Buongiorno" (Good morning) or "Buonasera" (Good evening) are the typical greetings.

Consider the Formalities: While Sardinians are courteous, they are more formal than other sections of Italy. Until you are asked to use first names, address individuals using titles like "Signore" (Mr.) or "Signora" (Ms.).

The Importance of "Grazie" (Thank you) and "Prego" (You're Welcome): Expressing appreciation is essential. A genuine "Grazie" goes a long way, and "Prego" is the proper answer to both gratitude and welcome.

Table Manners: Dining with Sardinian Flair

Sardinians take mealtimes seriously. Lunch is usually the biggest meal of the day and is eaten slowly. Respect the pace and enjoy the experience.

- **Formal surroundings, Informal Customs:** Although restaurant surroundings might be formal, the ambiance is often informal. It is okay if people talk loudly and linger over their meals.
- **Accept the Antipasti:** Sardinian dinners often start with a selection of antipasti (appetizers). Share them with your buddies and try a little of everything.
- **Bread Basket Etiquette:** Bread is a fixture on Sardinian tables. It is considered disrespectful to consume it alone before the main meal comes. After finishing your dinner, use bread to soak up any sauces.
- **Wine & Toasting:** Wine is a popular addition to meals. Wait for the host to propose a toast before lifting your glass. A simple "Salute" (Cheers) is sufficient.

Daily Life and Social Interaction:

Many stores and companies shut in the afternoon for a siesta break, which usually lasts between 1:00 and 4:00 p.m., so Schedule your errands accordingly.

- **Respect Personal Space:** Sardinians prefer to stand closer than other cultures during

interactions. Be cautious of personal space, but feel free to back away unduly.
- **The Art of Conversation:** Sardinians are proud of their island and like sharing their culture. Be an engaged listener and inquire about their customs and way of life. In general, political or religious discussions should be avoided in informal contexts.
- **Dress for the Occasion:** Sardinia has a laid-back atmosphere, particularly in coastal towns. When visiting churches or religious sites, dress modestly. Smarter attire is preferred at expensive restaurants and urban areas. When in doubt, choose a more conservative appearance.

Tips in Sardinia:

The tipping culture in Sardinia is developing. A little tip (5-10% of the bill) is often appreciated at restaurants, mainly if you have exceptional service. However, tipping is not required, and a simple "Grazie" can suffice at certain informal cafés and pubs. Tipping taxi drivers in tiny amounts is usual, and rounding up the fee is typical.

Celebrate Sardinian Traditions:

- **Respect Religious Festivities:** Sardinia celebrates several religious festivals throughout the year. If you see a parade, move aside and watch silently.

- **Dress Code for Churches:** Men and women should be modest when visiting churches. Cover your shoulders and knees.

Understanding and following these local traditions and etiquette can guarantee a smooth and pleasurable stay in Sardinia. Remember that a little effort goes a long way toward developing cultural interchange and producing memorable memories from your Sardinian vacation. So, embrace the spirit of "Sa Dou Sa" (local friendliness) and lose yourself in the island's allure!

3.3 Tips and Bargaining

Sardinia's breathtaking beauty and rich culture provide a memorable vacation experience. However, addressing financial issues like tipping and negotiation might take time in a new location. This detailed handbook will help you negotiate these situations with confidence and cultural sensitivity.

Tipping in Sardinia: A Delicate Dance.

The tipping culture in Sardinia is developing and varies according to the service and establishment. Here's a breakdown to help you navigate.

Restaurants: A little tip (5-10% of the bill) is always appreciated, mainly if you experience excellent service. However, tipping is not required. A tiny extra tip is optional if the service fee (coperto) is already included on the bill.

Taxis: It is usual practice for taxi drivers to round up their fares. You may also leave a modest tip (a few euros) for exemplary service or help with baggage.

Hotels: Tipping hotel employees such as porters or housekeepers is not required, but a modest token of gratitude (a few euros) is always acceptable.

Tipping is not anticipated in casual cafés or pubs. However, leaving some extra cash or rounding up your payment is a kind gesture.

General Tips for Tipping:

- **Consider the Service:** The quality of service is the most crucial element when deciding whether to tip. If the service was excellent, a modest tip will express your gratitude.
- **Pay with cash:** Because tipping is not required, bringing modest money enables you to pay discreetly when you want to.
- When in doubt, err on caution: A tiny gesture of thanks is always preferable to no gratuity. However, don't feel obligated to tip excessively.

Bargaining in Sardinia: Not the norm.

Bargaining, although popular in certain places of the globe, is different in Sardinia. Prices at businesses, restaurants, and services are usually set. But there are a few exceptions:

Street marketplaces: Prices may vary at open-air marketplaces selling souvenirs or handcrafted items. A courteous request for a little discount, particularly if you purchase numerous goods, is acceptable.
Unique Circumstances: In rare situations, if you're buying a high-value item from a local artist or antique shop, you may be able to negotiate the price. The trick is to remain courteous while avoiding pushy negotiation methods.

General Tips for Negotiation:

- **Be Polite and Respectful:** An excellent discussion and genuine interest in the product will go a long way. Avoid being forceful or demanding.
- **Do Your Research:** Before contacting the vendor, consider the item's reasonable worth.
- **Prepare to Walk Away:** If the vendor refuses to bargain, thank them respectfully and go away. There may be more solutions available.

Embrace Sardinian hospitality

While tipping and negotiating may be an issue, remember that Sardinians are recognized for their excellent hospitality. The genuine friendships you make and the cultural experiences you seek will likely be more satisfying than saving a few cents.

Following these principles and valuing cultural awareness will allow you to confidently negotiate tipping and negotiating situations in Sardinia, resulting in a smooth and pleasurable tour of this beautiful island.

3.4 Health and Safety Information

Sardinia is enticed by its breathtaking scenery, rich history, and dynamic culture. While safety is crucial for every tourist, a little planning may guarantee a worry-free and healthy exploration of this intriguing island. Here's a thorough health and safety checklist to help you relax and concentrate on having beautiful experiences in Sardinia.

Healthcare in Sardinia:

Medical Facilities: Sardinia has an extensive network of public hospitals and clinics. Major towns and cities have pharmacies (Pharmacia) that are well-stocked with medications.
Travel Insurance: It is strongly advised to have travel insurance that includes medical coverage. This guarantees that you will obtain appropriate medical treatment in the event of an emergency. Ensure your insurance covers planned activities, such as water sports or trekking.
Emergency Numbers: Keep emergency contact information on your phone. The emergency number for medical emergencies in Italy is 118.

Vaccination and Precautions:

Recommended vaccines: While no vaccines are required for admission into Sardinia, it is advisable to be current on basic immunizations such as tetanus, measles, and diphtheria. Consult your doctor or a travel clinic well before your trip to Sardinia to discover if further vaccines are required.

Mosquitoes may be prevalent, particularly during the summer months. Pack bug repellent with DEET and consider wearing long sleeves and trousers in the evenings to reduce bites.

Sun Safety: Sardinia has plenty of sunlight. To avoid sunburn, regularly use sunscreen with an SPF of 30 or higher, wear a helmet, and seek shade during peak sun hours.

Hydration: Staying hydrated is essential, particularly during the hot Sardinian summer. Carry a reusable water bottle and refill it regularly.

Safety Tips for Travelers:

Petty theft, such as bag snatching or pickpocketing, may happen in congested settings like tourist sites or public transit. Stay careful, keep your things safe, and avoid carrying too much cash.

Swimming Safety:
1. Only swim on approved beaches with lifeguards on duty.
2. Be wary of currents and follow any posted warnings.
3. See a local lifeguard for guidance if you need more clarification about the circumstances.

Hiking Safety: If you want to hike, particularly in isolated places, notify someone of your route and expected return time. Wear adequate footwear, pack plenty of drinks, and be mindful of possible risks such as loose rocks or uneven ground.
Wildfires may occur during the dry summer months. Be careful of fire limits and adhere to local standards.

Additional considerations:

- **Food and Water Safety:** Drink only bottled water, particularly while traveling outside of big cities. Avoid street food sellers and eat at reputed eateries that provide freshly prepared dishes.

- **Traffic Safety:** Italian motorists may be pushy. Crossing roadways, particularly outside established crosswalks, should be done with caution. If you want to hire a vehicle, acquaint yourself with traffic rules and road signs.

- Respect the local laws and traditions. Dress modestly while visiting churches and religious places. Be aware of noise levels, particularly in residential areas.

Following some essential health and safety precautions may give you a worry-free and pleasurable vacation in Sardinia. Remember, a little planning goes a long way toward ensuring your safety and enabling you to experience this intriguing island's charm.

3.5 Packing Essentials for Your Trip

Sardinia, a treasure trove of enthralling scenery, rich history, and lively culture, awaits discovery. However, a well-planned packing list is essential for a comfortable and happy trip before departing on your Sardinian adventure. Here's a complete guide to packing necessities for everything you need without going overboard.

Clothing for Every Season:

Sardinia's climate changes with the season. Here's a breakdown that can help you pack efficiently:

Summer (June-August):

1. Pack lightweight, breathable apparel such as cotton or linen t-shirts, shorts, sundresses, and swimsuits.
2. Pack a light sweater or jacket for chilly nights and windy seaside places. Remember

3. your hat, sunglasses, and comfortable walking footwear.

Shoulder Seasons (April-May & September-October):

1. Pack layers to accommodate changing temperatures.
2. Include long-sleeved shirts, light pants, and a multipurpose jacket.
3. Choose comfy closed-toe shoes that are ideal for walking.

Spring and fall (March and November): Pack warmer and lighter apparel layers. Pack a light rain jacket in case of an unexpected rainfall. Comfortable, closed-toe shoes are needed.

Essentials for Every Season:

Comfortable Walking Shoes: Sardinia has attractive villages, gorgeous hiking paths, and stunning coasts. Pack a firm and comfy pair of walking shoes for navigating various terrains.

Beach Gear (Optional): If you intend to spend time at the beach, bring a swimsuit, a beach towel, and a hat. Sunscreen, sunglasses, and water shoes are also necessary for sun and beach safety.

Personal Toiletries: Pack your usual toiletries, but consider the packing constraints, particularly for carry-on baggage. Consider using travel-sized containers to conserve room.

Pack a basic first-aid pack that includes medications for headaches, upset stomachs, bug bites, and minor wounds.

Additional considerations:

Dress Code for Religious Sites: To respect local norms, wear clothes covering your shoulders and knees while visiting churches or religious sites.

Evening Attire: Although Sardinia has a relaxed attitude, certain restaurants in wealthy neighborhoods or city centers may have a little dressier dress code. Pack multipurpose clothing for these situations.

Gadgets and Entertainment: Bring your phone, charger, and other required gadgets. Consider downloading e-books, movies, or music to entertain yourself while traveling. Depending on the kind of plug in your native country, you may need a universal adaptor.

Packing Tips for Efficiency:

- Roll, don't fold: Rolling garments save space and reduce wrinkles.

- **Pack Versatile Clothing:** Choose pieces that can be combined and matched to form numerous ensembles.

- Packing cubes help you arrange your items and better use the space in your bag.
- **Check Airline Restrictions:** Review your airline's baggage limit and weight restrictions for checked and carry-on bags to prevent surprise airport costs.

Remember that packing light offers you more flexibility and freedom of mobility on your Sardinian excursion. Following these guidelines and packing basics will guarantee a pleasant and worry-free tour of this enchanting island paradise.

Part 2: Exploring Sardinia by Region

Chapter 4: Breathtaking Coasts

4.1 Costa Smeralda: Luxury, Beaches, and Glamor

4.1.1 Must-see Beaches in Costa Smeralda

"The soul is not tied to where it resides, but where it travels." - Anonymous;

Explore Sardinia's breathtaking coastline, where the green waves of the Costa Smeralda (green Coast) lap against pristine white sand beaches. This refuge for luxury visitors and beach lovers has a network of secret coves, stunning rock formations, and a pulsating energy that will take your breath away. Pack your swimwear, sunscreen, and spirit of adventure as we visit some of Costa Smeralda's must-see beaches:

Cala Brandinchi, nicknamed *"Little Tahiti"* because of its striking similarity to the Polynesian island, is a beautiful wonder. The fine, fluffy sand resembles confectioners' sugar and the blue ocean shimmers beneath the Mediterranean sun. Relax on the beach, enjoy a refreshing swim, or explore the nearby granite rock formations, relics of an ancient environment.

Cala Brandinchi on Costa Smeralda, Sardinia.

Cala Mariolu is a remote paradise that can only be reached by boat or a challenging climb. The beach, a cove surrounded by spectacular cliffs, has pebbles and pink sand lapped by crystal-clear seas in a fascinating palette of turquoise and sapphire. Cala Mariolu is a snorkeler's paradise filled with vibrant marine life.

Cala Mariolu on Costa Smeralda, Sardinia.

Spiaggia del Principe (Prince's Beach): Located near the Cala di Volpe beach, Spiaggia del Principe is popular with celebrities and nobility. The beach is a paradise of smooth sand and clear water, perfect for swimming, sunbathing, and stand-up paddleboarding. Luxury resorts flank the Coast, providing upmarket facilities and beautiful vistas.

Spiaggia del Principe in Costa Smeralda, Sardinia.

Cala Liscia Ruja is ideal for families, with a small, protected bay and tranquil waves suitable for young children. The beach has a modest slope, which allows for safe paddling and swimming. It is a handy and attractive beach retreat with fine sand and services like sunbed and umbrella rentals.

Cala del Cavolo, a horseshoe-shaped bay surrounded by thick flora, provides a picturesque getaway. The beach is a mixture of sand and stones, caressed by lovely blue waves. Watersports aficionados may go kayaking, windsurfing, or diving, while others can rest on the beach and enjoy the beauty of their surroundings.

Cala del Cavolo on Costa Smeralda, Sardinia.

Beyond these must-see destinations, the Costa Smeralda coastline reveals secret coves and beaches begging to be explored. As you go, practice sustainable tourism by respecting the fragile ecosystem, appropriately disposing of garbage, and avoiding overcrowding in remote regions. With its spectacular beauty and limitless opportunities for leisure and entertainment, the Costa Smeralda offers an amazing Sardinian trip.

4.1.2 Towns and Villages To Explore

The Costa Smeralda, with its green seas and immaculate beaches, is undoubtedly appealing. But this charming location on Sardinia's northeastern edge offers more than simply lovely expanses of beach. Travel inland to find lovely towns and villages, each with its distinct personality and cultural tapestry. So, buckle up and prepare to explore:

Porto Cervo is Costa Smeralda's crown gem, serving as a playground for the wealthy and well-known. Luxurious boats bob in the port, luxury stores line the cobblestone walkways, and premium restaurants tantalize the senses. People watch the famous Piazzetta (little plaza) or go shopping for luxury. In the evening, the mood changes, with bustling nightlife and a hint of elegance in the air.

Porto Cervo, Costa Smeralda, Sardinia.

Porto Rotondo: Nestled in a lovely cove, Porto Rotondo provides a more tranquil alternative to the bustling energy of Porto Cervo. Pastel-colored buildings fall down the slope, framing a picturesque harbor.

Explore the charming boutiques and art galleries, eat excellent seafood at a waterfront restaurant, or relax on the beach and enjoy the laid-back environment.

Porto Rotondo, Costa Smeralda, Sardinia.

San Pantaleo: Escape the beach crowd and explore the heart of Gallura, a historical area in northern Sardinia. San Pantaleo, a picturesque community built on a hill, looks into a more traditional way of life. Wander through little lanes dotted with artisan stores and workshops, have a tasty supper at a local trattoria, or take in the panoramic views from the central plaza. Take advantage of the bustling market on Thursday mornings, which is brimming with local crafts, fresh food, and Sardinian delicacies.

San Pantaleo on Costa Smeralda, Sardinia.

Baja Sardinia: This beach resort town provides an ideal balance of rest and activity. Relax on the gorgeous beach, surrounded by aromatic juniper trees, or explore the nearby coves by kayak or boat. For a taste of history, go to the adjacent Nuragic archeological site, which offers an intriguing peek into Sardinia's ancient past. Enjoy a great supper at a beachside restaurant while the sun sets.

Baja Sardinia, Costa Smeralda, Sardinia

Arzachena, rich in history and culture, is the pulsating center of the Gallura area. Discover the town's rich history at the National Archaeological Museum, which houses antiquities from the Nuragic and Roman eras. Explore the massive granite outcrops known as the Roccia del Fungo (Mushroom Rock) or the Tomba dei Giganti (Giants' Tomb), a megalithic structure from the Bronze Age. Walking around the bustling town center in the evenings, dotted with stores, cafés, and restaurants.

Arzachena in Costa Smeralda, Sardinia.

This is only a sample of the intriguing towns and villages on the Costa Smeralda. Exploring beyond the beaches, you'll encounter a land rich in history, culture, and genuine Sardinian character. So, put on your walking shoes, embrace the spirit of exploration, and prepare to be amazed by the hidden gems of this unique place.

4.1.3 Activities and Daytrips

The Costa Smeralda shimmers with blue seas and gorgeous beaches, but there's a whole world waiting to be discovered beyond the shore. This exciting location provides diverse activities and day excursions, ideal for those seeking adventure, cultural immersion, or a taste of the great outdoors. So, unleash your inner adventurer and prepare to discover:

Sailing Adventure:
1. Set sail on the Costa Smeralda's green seas and discover the island's splendor from a new viewpoint.
2. Charter a private boat or join a guided excursion to see secret coves, spectacular cliffs, and isolated beaches.
3. Take a refreshing swim in hidden coves, snorkel among colorful marine life, or relax on deck and soak up the sun.

Many sailing experiences include lunch or snacks on board, making them ideal for spending a calm and memorable day at sea.

Archipelago Cruise: The Maddalena Archipelago, a group of islands north of the Costa Smeralda, is a paradise waiting to be discovered. Take a day excursion by boat or a guided cruise to visit a chain of islands noted for their pink granite outcrops, crystal-clear seas, and immaculate beaches. Spend time on the car-free island of Maddalena, exploring the quaint port town or hiking to the island's summit for stunning vistas. Spargi Island has isolated coves perfect for swimming and snorkeling. At the same time, Budelli Island is noted for its "Spiaggia Rosa" (Pink Beach), which has sand-tinted a delicate rose hue by microscopic coral pieces.

Image of Archipelago Cruise at Costa Smeralda, Sardinia.

Off-Road trip: An off-road trip allows you to explore the rough beauty of the Sardinian landscape. Join a guided Jeep trip or hire an ATV to explore secret paths, drive past vineyards and olive orchards, and find lovely communities unspoiled by mass tourists. This fascinating experience enables you to see stunning views, meet local shepherds and their flocks, and better understand the island's natural beauty and traditional way of life.

Image of Offroad Adventure at Costa Smeralda, Sardinia.

Wine Tasting Tour: Sardinia has an excellent winemaking legacy, and the Gallura area, which includes the Costa Smeralda, is no exception. Take a wine-tasting tour and learn about the island's unique grape varieties and traditional winemaking processes. Visit a local vineyard to learn about the production process from enthusiastic winemakers and sample Vermentino, Cannonau, and other area favorites. Combine your wine tasting with a delightful meal of local cheeses, cured meats, and fresh Sardinian bread for a memorable gastronomic experience.

Archaeological Gems: Sardinia's history spans thousands of years, and the Costa Smeralda area is no exception. Explore the island's history by visiting excellent archeological sites. Explore the Nuragic ruins, intriguing stone buildings from the Bronze Age dispersed around the area. The Nuragic Complex at Arzachena, a UNESCO World Heritage Site, provides insight into this ancient culture. Visit the Tombs of the Giants, which are megalithic tombs that highlight the Nuragic people's extraordinary technical achievements. These historical places provide a glimpse into Sardinia's exciting history and an opportunity to engage with the island's deeply ingrained culture.

The Costa Smeralda has something for everyone. So, whether you're looking for an adrenaline-pumping adventure, cultural immersion, or a quiet exploration of nature's beauty, a day excursion or activity is ready to make unforgettable memories in this stunning Sardinian paradise.

4.2 The Rugged North: Alghero, Stintino, and the Asinara Islands

4.2.1 Stunning Beaches and Natural Beauty

"The soul is not tied to where it resides, but where it travels." - Anonymous;

Sardinia's northern shore entices with a mesmerizing combination of history, culture, and natural beauty. Beyond the Costa Smeralda, explore the riches of Alghero, Stintino, and the Asinara Archipelago, each offering distinct experiences and spectacular vistas. So, buckle up and prepare to explore:

Alghero: A Catalan Tapestry by the Sea.

Step into Alghero, a lovely town with strong Catalan influences, for a one-of-a-kind cultural experience. Wander around the old center's small lanes, admiring the honey-colored stone houses and hearing the beautiful tones of inhabitants speaking Catalan. Take advantage of the majestic 14th-century walls that previously defended the town and provide breathtaking shore views.

Image of Alghero, Sardinia.

Escape the noon heat and explore the interesting Neptune's Grotto. Take a guided boat trip through a network of sea caverns filled with stalactites, stalagmites, and dazzling rock formations. Marvel at the Grotta di luce (Grotto of Light), a cavern lighted by a natural aperture that creates a stunning display of light and water.

Image of Neptune's Grotto in Alghero, Sardinia

After exploring, relax on one of Alghero's stunning beaches. Lido San Giovanni is a popular option, a horseshoe-shaped bay with beautiful sand and crystal-clear seas. For a pinch of privacy, visit Cala Luna Longa, a secret cove accessible by boat, or a picturesque stroll that provides a refuge of serenity among spectacular cliffs.

Image of Lido San Giovanni in Alghero, Sardinia

Stintino: Paradise Found.

Prepare to be captivated by the natural beauty of Stintino, a peninsula noted for its white sand beaches and clear seas. La Pelosa Beach, typically named among Italy's most beautiful, offers unbelievably pure water, smooth sand that feels like flour between your toes, and an island called Isola della Pelosa (Pelosa Island), which may be reached by wading through shallow water.

Image of Isola della Pelosa in Stintino, Sardinia.

Image of La Pelosa Beach in Stintino, Sardinia.

A boat excursion allows you to explore the beautiful hues of the Stintino shoreline. Consider Cala Brandinchi, a beach known as "Little Tahiti" because of its excellent sand and shallow blue waves that resemble the Polynesian island. Cala del Covo, surrounded by stunning cliffs and rich flora, is a quiet paradise for swimming and snorkeling.

The Asinara Archipelago: A Sanctuary of Nature

Set sail toward the Asinara Archipelago, a national park renowned for its untouched beauty and diverse wildlife. The largest island, Asinara, was previously a prison colony but is now a protected habitat for uncommon animals like albino donkeys and wild boar. Explore the island by bike or on foot, trek to the highest point for spectacular views, or dive in crystal-clear seas teaming with marine life.

Cala Reale, a horseshoe-shaped bay with shallow blue seas and a fine sand and pebble beach, invites you to breathe in the pure sea air and relax. You can relax on the beach, have a picnic lunch in the shade of juniper trees, or explore the nearby coves by kayak.

Image of Cala Reale, Asinara Archipelago, Sardinia

Alghero, Stintino, and the Asinara Archipelago provide a compelling blend of cultural immersion, spectacular natural beauty, and excellent beach experiences. So, put on your walking shoes, pack your swimwear, and prepare to explore Sardinia's hidden gems on the northwestern shore.

4.2.2 Exploring Historic Alghero.

Alghero, a beautiful Sardinian town tucked along the northern Coast, entices with its combination of history, culture, and lively energy. Wander through its picturesque streets and be taken back in time as you encounter relics of its rich history, Catalan influences, and a strong feeling of Sardinian identity. So, take your walking shoes and prepare to explore:

Immerse Yourself in Catalan Charm: Enter the old heart of Alghero and be surprised with a maze of tiny streets lined with honey-colored stone houses. These architectural jewels tell stories about the town's intriguing past. Catalan sovereignty over Alghero lasted centuries, and their impact can be seen in the language, architecture, and even street names. As you wander, keep an ear out for the melodic tones of Catalan spoken by certain inhabitants, which are a lovely reminder of the town's distinct origin.

Image of Alghero's medieval center, Sardinia.

Guardians of Time: The Fortifications Alghero's magnificent 14th-century fortifications reflect the city's stormy history. Walk around the walls and see the well-preserved turrets and bastions that previously defended the town from attackers. Climb the Torre di Porta Terra (Porta Terra Tower), the central ancient town entryway, for stunning coastline and port views. As you stand atop the walls, envision the busy port activities and deadly wars that formed Alghero's past.

Torre di Porta Terra in Alghero, Sardinia

A Cathedral Rich in History: The Cathedral of Santa Maria Immaculate, a masterpiece of Gothic-Catalan architecture, is a must-see for every history enthusiast. Step inside to see the towering nave, elaborate stained-glass windows, and a stunning altarpiece Featuring moments from the Virgin Mary's life. Take advantage of the neighboring Coral Museum, which has a one-of-a-kind collection of Sardinian coral jewelry and artifacts that reflect the island's long history of craftsmanship.

Image of Cathedral of Santa Maria Immaculate in Alghero, Sardinia

Discover Alghero's Underground Secrets:
1. Enter the enthralling realm of the Grotta di Nettuno (Neptune's Grotto).
2. Take a guided boat trip through a network of sea caverns filled with stalactites, stalagmites, and dazzling rock formations.
3. Marvel at the Grotta di luce (Grotto of Light), a cavern lighted by a natural aperture that creates a stunning display of light and water. The cold grotto air will be a pleasant relief from the Sardinian summer heat.

Image of Grotta di Nettuno in Alghero, Sardinia

A Cultural Tapestry: Alghero's cultural landscape is a lively blend of Catalan traditions and Sardinian flare. Attend the annual Alghero Catalan Festival, which takes place in August, to immerse yourself in local culture. Witness vibrant parades, traditional music performances, and residents dressed in extravagant costumes. Throughout the year, please watchanfeyetreet performers, art shows, and local artisans displaying their work. Alghero's rich tapestry is sure to make an indelible impact.

Alghero's ancient charm, an intriguing combination of cultures, and hidden jewels await discovery. Walking through its streets, you'll find a town where the past whispers secrets around every corner, and the present hums with vitality. So start your Alghero tour and let yourself be fascinated by this fantastic Sardinian gem.

4.2.3 Boat Trips to Asinara National Park.

The Asinara National Park, located off Sardinia's northwestern Coast, entices visitors with its beautiful beaches, crystal-clear seas, and diverse species. While some regions of the island are off-limits to preserve its natural beauty, boat tours provide an unparalleled opportunity to see the park's marvels. Pack your bikini, sunscreen, and spirit of adventure, and prepare to set sail for paradise!

Choosing Your Asinara National Park Boat Tour:

Asinara National Park provides a range of boat excursion alternatives to suit various interests and budgets. Here's a simple guide to help you find the ideal experience.

Full-Day Adventure: Take a boat tour through Asinara National Park to see its natural splendor. These cruises usually leave from Stintino, a lovely village on the Sardinian mainland. You'll spend the day cruising around the Asinara coast, stopping at hidden coves to swim, snorkel, and sunbathe. Lunch is often included, either on board or at a seaside restaurant. Watch for dolphins and other marine life while navigating the crystal-clear seas.

Full-Day Boat Trip to Asinara National Park in Sardinia.

Half-Day Exploration: A half-day boat tour is an excellent choice for those with limited time. These trips glimpse Asinara's magnificence, with pauses for swimming and snorkeling in some of the park's most picturesque coves. Half-day excursions are great for families with small children or those looking to combine their Asinara experience with other activities in Sardinia.

Sailing Adventure: Discover the majesty of Asinara National Park from the deck of a sailboat. These private trips provide an opportunity to unwind and appreciate the beauty of the Sardinian coastline. Learn the fundamentals of sailing from the expert skipper, or relax and enjoy the journey. Sailing cruises often include swimming and snorkeling breaks, making them ideal for exploring Asinara's underwater ecosystem.

What to Expect During Your Boat Trip:

Once you've decided on a boat tour, here's what you can expect:

Departing the port: Feel the thrill as you sail from Stintino's lively port. As you leave the mainland behind, take at the spectacular cliffs and secluded bays that skirt the Sardinian Coast. Look out for colorful fishing boats and luxury yachts in the turquoise seas.

Cruising along the Asinara Coastline: The boat ride itself is an experience. Relax on deck and take in the Mediterranean sunlight as the skipper navigates the crystal-clear waters. Feel the cold sea wind on your skin and take in the untouched beauty of Asinara National Park as it unfolds before you.

Swimming and Snorkeling in Paradise: One of the attractions of each Asinara National Park boat tour is the chance to swim and snorkel in crystal-clear seas. The park has isolated coves with calm, shallow waters perfect for families with little children. For more daring swimmers, deeper places are abounding with vibrant marine life. Don your mask and fins and explore the aquatic environment, looking for fish, coral reefs, and other hidden treasures.

Exploring Secluded Coves: The Asinara National Park shoreline is filled with secret coves that can only be

Accessed by boat. Your skipper will take you to some of the park's most stunning locations, where you may rest on pristine beaches, explore rocky outcrops, or enjoy the peacefulness of these hidden havens.

Learning about the Park's History and Ecology: The captain or a park ranger often provides insightful comments during boat rides. Discover the intriguing history of Asinara National Park, a former prison colony now a wildlife sanctuary. Learn about the park's unique ecology and the continuing conservation efforts to preserve its natural beauty.

A boat voyage to Asinara National Park is more than a trek; it's an unforgettable experience. Set sail for adventure and experience the enchantment of this unique Sardinian gem.

4.3 Scenic East Coast: Ogliastra and the Baunei Mountains.

4.3.1: Dramatic Landscapes and Hidden Coves

Sardinia's eastern pulse beats at a chaotic pace. Ogliastra, a territory shaped by time and wind, reveals stunning scenery, secret coves with breathtakingly blue seas, and lovely settlements steeped in history. The Baunei Mountains, a jagged spine that divides the area, provide limitless options for adventure. So, lace up your hiking boots, grab your bikini, and prepare to experience a less-visited Sardinia:

Cala Goloritze is Nature's Sculptural Masterpiece.

Take a picturesque stroll or boat cruise to reach Cala Goloritze, a cove known for its dramatic beauty. Towering limestone cliffs, carved by wind and water over millennia, surround a beach of flawless pebbles lapped by blue waves. A famous natural archway, the "Goloritze Portal," is a tribute to nature's beauty. Take a soothing plunge in the calm water, swim to secret caves, or sit on the beach and enjoy the natural magnificence.

Image of Cala Goloritze in Ogliastra, Sardinia

Trek Through the Selvaggio Blu: A Path for the Determined - The Selvaggio Blu (Wild Blue) path calls out to experienced hikers looking for adventure. This arduous multi-day trek follows the Baunei coastline, mounting cliffs, passing through juniper woods, and rewarding hikers with stunning views of the jagged coastline. Camping beneath a starry sky and waking up to the sound of breaking waves is an unforgettable experience. Remember: the Selvaggio Blu is not for the faint of heart. A safe and memorable expedition requires proper preparation, fitness, and a skilled guide.

Image of Selvaggio Blu path near Ogliastra, Sardinia

Baunei: A Village Steeped in Tradition - Nestled among rolling hills, Baunei looks into a more traditional way of life. Wander through small alleyways lined with stone cottages, marvel at the artistry of the 16th-century Church of San Nicola di Bari, and enjoy great local food at a family-run trattoria. Take advantage of the weekly market, which has a colorful display of fresh fruit, local crafts, and the opportunity to connect with friendly folks.

Baunei is an excellent location for experiencing the natural splendor of Ogliastra and the Baunei Mountains.

Cala Mariolu: A Snorkeler's Paradise - Only accessible by boat or a strenuous climb, Cala Mariolu is a remote cove known for its pristine beauty. Imagine yourself on a beach surrounded by majestic cliffs. The cove has a distinct combination of pebbles and pink sand, lapped by crystal-clear waters in a stunning turquoise and sapphire color scheme. Cala Mariolu is a snorkeler's paradise, with colorful fish and other marine life rushing around the rocks. As you explore the underwater environment, remember to glance up and admire the sheer magnificence of the cliffs that soar above.

Image of Cala Mariolu in Ogliastra, Sardinia

Grotte del Bue Marino: A Journey Underground - Explore the enthralling world of the Grotte del Bue Marino (Grotto of the Monk Seal). Take a guided boat trip through a network of sea caverns filled with stalactites, stalagmites, and dazzling rock formations. The cave receives its name from the monk seals that originally lived there. Marvel at the "Lake of Mirrors," a calm water reflecting the cave's spectacular formations, and visit the "Sala della Musica" (Hall of Music), where natural acoustics produce an otherworldly atmosphere.

Image of Grotte del Bue Marino near Ogliastra, Sardinia.

Ogliastra and the Baunei Mountains combine stunning vistas, secret coves, and a rich cultural history. Whether you're an experienced hiker, a beach bum, or an adventurer looking for off-the-beaten-path thrills, this mesmerizing location offers something for everyone. So, escape the crowd and experience the raw beauty of Ogliastra, where hidden treasures await discovery.

4.3.2 Hiking and Outdoor Activities.

Ogliastra, located on Sardinia's eastern coast, is an adventurer's paradise. Rugged mountains pierce the sky, turquoise seas lap at isolated coves, and old woods whisper secrets in the wind. So, put on your hiking boots, grab your rucksack, and prepare to enjoy the pleasure of outdoor activities in Ogliastra:

Conquer the Supramonte: A Hiker's Playground - Strap on your backpack and explore the Supramonte, a massive limestone plateau that dominates Ogliastra's scenery. Marked pathways weave through juniper trees, providing stunning views of the shore and valleys below. Challenge yourself on the Selvaggio Blu (Wild Blue) trek, a multi-day route ideal for experienced hikers, or choose shorter, beautiful excursions to appreciate the natural splendor at your leisure. Watch for golden eagles flying above and the rare mouflon sheep grazing on the rocky hillsides.

Spelunking Adventure: Grotte Su Marmuri - Journey into the earth's center to discover the Grotte Su Marmuri (Marmora Caves), Europe's sixth-longest cave system. Walk through a maze of rooms decorated with stalactites, stalagmites, and dazzling rock formations. Marvel at the "Sala della Regina" (Hall of the Queen), a cavern with stately columns, and take in the beautiful "Lake Coghinas," a crystal-clear water reflecting the cave's brilliant patterns. This spelunking expedition offers a one-of-a-kind opportunity to uncover Ogliastra's hidden treasures.

Image of Grotte Su Marmuri in Ogliastra, Sardinia.

Rock Climbing Paradise: Biddiris Gorge - Calling all thrill seekers! The Biddiris Gorge, a stunning canyon created by the Rio Flumineddu River, is ideal for rock climbers of all ability levels. Challenge yourself on various climbing routes, from cliffs to overhangs, all in a stunning natural environment. Experienced climbers may take on the legendary "Gola di Gorroppu" (Gorropu Gorge), Europe's deepest canyon, while novices can find plenty of introductory routes to test their abilities.

Image of Gola di Gorroppu in Ogliastra, Sardinia

Horseback Riding Through the Countryside - See the beauty of Ogliastra from a fresh perspective: on horseback! Join a guided horseback riding excursion to see undulating hills, secret valleys, and old routes. Imagine cantering through verdant woodlands, feeling the breeze in your hair and the horse's cadence under you. Horseback riding is an excellent pastime for families and nature enthusiasts, providing a unique opportunity to interact with the Ogliastra countryside.

Image of horseback riding in Ogliastra, Sardinia.

Canyoning Adventure: Su Gorroppu - For those looking for an adrenaline rush and stunning surroundings, canyoning in Su Gorroppu is a fantastic experience. Rappel down waterfalls, cross tiny valleys, and bathe in crystal-clear pools with professional guides. Su Gorroppu, Europe's deepest canyon, provides a challenging yet rewarding trip for those who want to overcome nature's barriers.

Image of canyoning at Su Gorroppu, Ogliastra, Sardinia

Ogliastra's diversified scenery entices outdoor lovers of all levels. Whether you like the difficulty of a multi-day walk, the excitement of rock climbing, or a leisurely horseback ride through the countryside, Ogliastra offers something for everyone. So, pack your spirit of adventure and prepare to explore the raw beauty of this alluring Sardinian area.

4.4 Southern Shores: Cagliari and Chia

4.4.1 Exploring the Vibrant Capital City, Cagliari.

"Travel makes one modest. You see what a tiny place you occupy in the world." - Gustave Flaubert:

Cagliari, Sardinia's bustling city, is alive with history, culture, and a hint of contemporary refinement. Carved onto a series of hills overlooking the Gulf of Cagliari, the city is a fascinating mix of ancient ruins, busy districts, and breathtaking coastline vistas. So, lace up your walking shoes, grab your camera, and prepare to explore:

Ascend to the Castello District: A Journey Through Time—Begin your Cagliari experience at the ancient center of the city. Stroll through narrow, cobblestone lanes surrounded by ancient towers and relics of the city's protective walls. Climb the Elephant Tower (Torre dell'Elefante) for a panoramic perspective of the city and port. Explore the Cagliari Cathedral, a magnificent example of Pisan architecture, and enjoy the beautiful carvings and artworks within. The Castello neighborhood is a treasure mine of history waiting to be discovered.

Image of Castello district in Cagliari, Sardinia.

Image of Elephant Tower in Cagliari, Sardinia

Image of Cagliari Cathedral on Sardinia.

The Basilica of San Saturnino is a hidden treasure in the Stampace area, so go beyond the usual tourist circuit to uncover it. This early Christian basilica from the 5th century has a distinct architectural style and a tranquil ambiance. Descend into the crypt, a remarkable archeological site with Roman and Punic ruins. The Basilica di San Saturnino provides insight into Cagliari's rich pastoral heritage.

Image of Basilica di San Saturnino in Cagliari, Sardinia

Museo Archeologico Nazionale: Unearthing Sardinia's Past - Discover Sardinia's rich past at the Museo Archeologico Nazionale (National Archaeological Museum). Explore a vast collection of items dating from the Neolithic to the Roman era. Admire the ornate Nuragic sculptures, the remains of a culture that flourished on the island thousands of years ago. The museum provides a well-curated trip through Sardinia's history, giving visitors a better grasp of the island's cultural heritage.

Cagliari's National Archaeological Museum

Image of Museo Archeologico Nazionale in Cagliari, Sardinia

Stroll through the Marina and Bastion of Saint Remy—Cagliari's ancient harbor. The Marina is a thriving center of activity. Watch colorful fishing boats bobbing in the port, appreciate the luxurious yachts docked nearby, and breathe in the pure sea air. As you meander down the promenade, go to the Bastion of Saint Remy, a star-shaped castle with breathtaking views of the city and shoreline. Enjoy a gelato or a refreshing drink at a seaside café while enjoying the vivid environment.

Image of Bastion of Saint Remy in Cagliari, Sardinia.

Image of Marina in Cagliari, Sardinia

Local & Cultural Delights: Explore Cagliari's Markets – Take in Cagliari's bustling markets' sights, sounds, and fragrances. The San Benedetto market contains fresh fruit, local crafts, and Sardinian delicacies. Sample cured meats, drink local solid coffee, and see the vibrant chatter between merchants and customers. In the evening, visit the bustling fish market at La Pescheria, where the day's fresh catch is exhibited on ice and glistens beneath the market lights.

Image of San Benedetto Market in Cagliari, Sardinia

Cagliari begs to be explored on foot. Wander through its lovely districts, find secret squares, and discover unexpected treats. The city's dynamic energy, rich history, and breathtaking coastline environment guarantee an outstanding experience for every visitor. So pack your luggage, embrace the spirit of adventure, and prepare to explore its charm.

4.4.2 Relaxing on Chia's Beautiful Beaches.

Sardinia's southern coasts call with the promise of complete leisure. Chia is a beautiful seaside community with a stretch of immaculate beaches, blue waters, and a relaxed ambiance ideal for relaxing. So, take your swimsuit, sunscreen, and beach blanket, and prepare to soak up the Sardinian sun:

Cala Cipolla: A Cove of Tranquility - Escape the crowd and find Cala Cipolla, a hidden treasure in a thick pine forest. This quiet cove has a beach of beautiful sand surrounded by calm blue waves. Relax on the beach and enjoy the peaceful sound of waves lapping on the coast. Take a pleasant plunge in the crystal-clear water, ideal for families with small children. For a sense of adventure, explore the neighboring rocky outcrops filled with marine life.

Image of Cala Cipolla in Chia, Sardinia

Cala Marina: Paradise Found - Prepare to be blown away by the splendor of Cala Marina. This crescent-shaped beach has incredibly white sand that feels like fluffy powder between your toes. The blue water here is shallow and quiet, perfect for swimming and snorkeling. Rent a sunbed and umbrella, or stretch out your beach towel under an umbrella to enjoy the Sardinian sun. Cala

Marina has a range of water sports activities, including kayaking, paddleboarding, and windsurfing, for those wanting a little more excitement.

Image of Cala Marina in Chia, Sardinia

Spiaggia di Chia: The Heart of the Action - The area's principal beach, Spiaggia di Chia, is a thriving hive of activity. This wide length of the beach has something for everyone. Families may construct sandcastles and splash in the shallow waves, while sunbathers can rest on comfy loungers and catch some sunshine. Beach volleyball courts, windsurfing rentals, and horseback riding options are available along the coast. Spiaggia di Chia also has a selection of pubs and restaurants that provide cool beverages and excellent meals only steps away from the beach.

Image of Spiaggia di Chia in Chia, Sardinia

Cala Luna: A Picturesque Escape—Cala Luna is a remote cove known for its dramatic beauty, and it can only be reached by boat or a picturesque stroll. Towering cliffs surround a beach with beautiful sand and crystal-clear seas. Discover secret grottoes accessible only by swimming, snorkel in brilliant coral reefs alive with marine life, or just rest on the beach and take in the calm of this quiet paradise.

Image of Cala Luna in Chia, Sardinia

Le Dune di Chia: A Natural Oasis - For a one-of-a-kind beach experience, go beyond the seashore to Le Dune di Chia (The Dunes of Chia). This protected area has an astonishing stretch of dunes that reach heights of up to 30 meters. Hike or cycle through this natural sanctuary, enjoying the fine sand under your feet and the pleasant sea wind on your skin. As you climb a dune, you'll be rewarded with spectacular panoramic views of the Chia coastline and surrounding scenery.

Image of Le Dune di Chia, Sardinia.

Chia's beaches provide something for any beachgoer. Chia offers it all, whether you want to relax in a private cove, visit a bustling beach with various activities, or explore unique natural scenery. So, pack your beach needs, enjoy the laid-back attitude, and prepare to be amazed by Chia's stunning beaches.

4.4.3 Archaeological sites and historical gems.

While Chia's stunning beaches may immediately draw attention, this charming Sardinian hamlet has a rich history that begs to be studied. Beyond the beach, you'll find a treasure trove of archeological sites, old ruins, and historical jewels that tell stories from bygone eras. So, put on your walking shoes, grab your hat, and prepare to start on a voyage through time:

Monte Longa's Nuragic Giants: Visit the archeological site of Monte Longa to learn about the intriguing Nuragic culture that existed thousands of years ago. These mystery people, who lived in Sardinia from the Bronze Age until the Roman period, created spectacular megalithic constructions known as nuraghi. Explore Monte Longa's partly excavated nuraghe, which features gigantic stone blocks and sophisticated building processes. As you stand among these ancient remains, consider the life and beliefs of the Nuragic people who constructed them.

Chiesa di San Nicola: A Spiritual Sanctuary - Nestled among rolling hills, the Chiesa di San Nicola (Church of Saint Nicholas) provides insight into Chia's pastoral heritage. This lovely 12th-century Romanesque church has a modest yet attractive front and a serene ambiance. Step inside to observe the wonderfully restored paintings representing Saint Nicholas' life. The church is a refuge of peace, ideal for a moment of thought while you explore Chia's historical riches.

Image of Chiesa di San Nicola in Chia, Sardinia

Watch for the Torre di Chia (Chia Tower), a Spanish watchtower built on a hill overlooking the seashore. This defensive tower, built in the 16th century during Spanish authority, acted as an observation post to safeguard the region from pirates and invaders. Climb to the top of the tower to enjoy panoramic views of the Chia coastline, surrounding farmland, and distant mountains. Imagine the troops stationed here centuries ago, watching over the blue waves and defending the Sardinian beaches.

Image of Spanish Watchtower at Chia, Sardinia.

The Museo del Modellino della Barca (Museum of the Boat Model) takes you deep into Chia's maritime legacy. This museum has a scale model of a classic Sardinian fishing boat, the "Navicella Sarda." Discover these boats' history and building skills, which local fishermen initially used to traverse Sardinian seas. The museum also has displays on traditional fishing methods and the significance of the sea to the local way of life.

Image of Museum of the Boat Model in Chia, Sardinia.

The Necropolis of Is Arutas, located a short drive from Chia, is an ancient cemetery dating back to the Phoenician and Punic eras (8th-3rd century BC). Explore the fantastic rock-cut tombs etched into the limestone cliffs, each providing insight into the ancient civilizations' burial habits. The cemetery is on a beautiful beach with white sand and turquoise waves, providing a unique blend of historical inquiry and coastal enjoyment.

Chia's historical sites provide a fascinating glimpse into the island's rich history. From the fascinating Nuragic past to the protective watchtowers and traditional fishing activities, each location reveals a piece of the tale that built this unique Sardinian community. So wear your walking shoes, embrace your inner explorer, and travel through time in Chia.

Part 3: Experience Sardinia

Chapter 5, Beaches and Water Activities

5.1 Snorkelling, Diving, and Water Sports Activities

"The sea, once it casts its spell, holds one in its net of wonder forever." - Jacques Cousteau:

Sardinia's beautiful seas and varied marine life entice divers of all abilities. From brilliant coral reefs filled with colorful fish to undiscovered shipwrecks whispering stories of the past, the island provides a world of adventure waiting to be discovered. Grab your snorkel, fins, or diving gear, and prepare to dive into the crystal-clear depths:

Snorkeling Paradise: The Marine Reserve of Capo Coda Cavallo - Put on your mask and fins and dive into the underwater paradise of the Capo Coda Cavallo Marine Reserve. This protected region, situated on Sardinia's northeastern point, is home to a diverse range of marine species. Swim with lively schools of fish, admire the beautiful hues of coral reefs, and uncover secret underwater tunnels teeming With life. The tranquil, shallow waters here are ideal for novice snorkelers, while more experienced explorers may travel farther out to see deeper reefs and shipwrecks.

Scuba Diving Adventures: The Secada Channel - Certified divers must explore the Secada Channel, which separates the islands of Asinara and Stintino. This waterway is known for its powerful currents, which attract a variety of marine species. As you explore the underwater environment, you will likely encounter playful dolphins, magnificent manta rays, and perhaps elusive whale sharks. The Secada Channel also has a fascinating underwater cemetery, with shipwrecks from all periods lying on the seafloor, each whispering stories about their previous adventures.

Image of Scuba Diving in Secada Channel, Sardinia

Windsurfing Paradise: La Saline Beach - If you want to experience the excitement of riding the waves, visit La Saline Beach on the island's southern shore. This beach is a sanctuary for windsurfers of all abilities, with constant winds and ideal wave conditions. Rent your equipment or take lessons from skilled instructors, and enjoy the thrill of gliding over the turquoise waves with the wind in your hair. La Saline Beach also provides beautiful views of the coastline, providing a unique experience.

Image of windsurfing in La Saline Beach, Sardinia

Kitesurfing Adventures: Porto Pollo Bay - For adrenaline seekers looking for an exciting adventure, kitesurfing at Porto Pollo Bay is a must-do. This picturesque harbor on Sardinia's northern coast features solid winds and flat seas, perfect for kitesurfing. Harness the strength of the wind as you glide over the ocean, feeling the spray on your face and the rush of defying gravity. Beginners may take lessons, while experienced kitesurfers can challenge themselves and try dangerous maneuvers.

Image of Kitesurfing at Porto Pollo Bay, Sardinia

Stand-Up Paddleboarding: Exploring Hidden Coves— Stand-up paddleboarding (SUP) is a great way to relax and explore Sardinia's coastline. Rent a SUP board and paddle around the tranquil waves, admiring the splendor of quiet coves, secret beaches, and majestic cliffs. SUP is an excellent way to get some fitness while seeing the breathtaking environment. Try SUP yoga, which combines a workout with the peacefulness of the water.

Image of stand-up paddleboarding in Sardinia.

Sardinia's waterways provide many opportunities for exploration and adventure. Whether you're a seasoned diver looking for underwater thrills, a beginning snorkeler admiring the beauty of the coral reefs, or a water sports fanatic needing an adrenaline rush, Sardinia offers something for everyone. So, pack your swimwear, enjoy the crystal-clear seas, and be ready to explore the enchantment of the undersea world.

5.2 Boat Tours and Sail Trips

Sardinia is more than simply a beach getaway; it is a mariner's heaven. The island's rugged coastline, dotted with hidden coves and secret beaches, reveals its absolute splendor when explored from the ocean. Set sail on a boat tour or an exciting sailing adventure, and prepare to explore Sardinia's hidden beauties.

La Maddalena Archipelago: Island Hopping Adventure - Take a boat trip to the La Maddalena Archipelago, a group of islands north of Sardinia. Cruise past Budelli's pink granite cliffs, see the turquoise seas of Cala Mariolu and discover the lovely village of La Maddalena. Stop for a relaxing dip in a hidden bay, dive amid brilliant coral reefs alive with life, and have a wonderful lunch aboard while admiring spectacular archipelago views. Boat cruises are a simple and comfortable way to see the archipelago's attractions, enabling you to quickly bounce from island to island.

Boat trip of La Maddalena Archipelago in Sardinia.

Sail the Gulf of Orosei: A Journey of Dramatic Coastlines - Set sail on an exciting day cruise around Sardinia's east coast, the Gulf of Orosei. Admire towering limestone cliffs carved by wind and water, find secluded coves accessible only by boat, and explore sea caverns studded with stalactites and stalagmites. Take a relaxing plunge in the turquoise waters of Cala Goloritze, a private beach enclosed by a natural archway, or snorkel among the colorful fish at Cala Mariolu. Sailing cruises in the Gulf of Orosei provide a new perspective on the island's rough beauty, as well as the Opportunity to find hidden jewels that are not accessible by land.

Sailing expedition around the Gulf of Orosei in Sardinia.

Sunset cruise over the Costa Smeralda: A Touch of Luxury - Enjoy a luxury sunset cruise over Sardinia's glittering coastline. Board a beautiful boat and sail past Porto Cervo, a billionaire's playground, marvel at the emerald green seas and quiet bays, and watch the sky light up with brilliant hues as the sun sets below the horizon. Enjoy great snacks and beverages aboard and the sheer luxury atmosphere as you cruise around this breathtaking coastline. Sunset cruises along the Costa Smeralda are a romantic and unique opportunity to appreciate Sardinia's splendor.

Sunset sail on the Costa Smeralda, Sardinia.

Dolphin-watching expedition: Encountering Marine Mammals—Set off on a fantastic expedition searching for dolphins in the seas off Sardinia. Climb onto a comfy boat and sail out to sea, watching for lively dolphin pods jumping across the water. Witness these gorgeous animals in their native environment and learn about their habits from the trained marine scientists on board. Dolphin-watching cruises are ideal for families and nature enthusiasts, providing an opportunity to have lifelong experiences.

Dolphin Watching Adventure in Sardinia

Set sail on a catamaran excursion to Asinara National Park, a protected island off Sardinia's northwest coast, to explore a pristine paradise. Explore the island's beautiful beaches, climb across its rocky terrain, and see a variety of flora and animals. Take a relaxing plunge in the crystal-clear waters of Cala Reale, a quiet beach renowned for its beauty, or snorkel amid bright coral reefs brimming with life. Catamaran trips to Asinara National Park allow you to avoid the crowd and enjoy the natural beauty of this unique island.

Sardinia's waterways provide limitless opportunities for exploration. Whether you choose a sumptuous sailing excursion along the beautiful Costa Smeralda, a thrilling adventure in search of dolphins, or a voyage of discovery through the spectacular landscapes of the Gulf of Orosei, there's a boat tour or sailing trip ready to make your Sardinian vacation memorable. So set sail, feel the sea wind in your hair, and explore Sardinia's charm from a different viewpoint.

Chapter 6: Exploring History and Culture.

6.1 Nuragic Culture and Archaeological Sites

Sardinia is a beautiful island in the Mediterranean Sea with a long and complicated history. One of the most intriguing parts of this narrative is about the Nuragic civilization, a Bronze Age society that flourished on the island from about 1800 BC to 238 BC. These mysterious individuals left behind a magnificent legacy: the nuraghe, towering stone structures that continue perplexing archaeologists and piquing people's interest today.

Who Were The Nuragic People?

The Nuragic people's origins and everyday lives remain mysterious, with continuous inquiry and discussion. Scholars think they originated in the Iberian Peninsula or mainland Italy, bringing superior metalworking methods and a distinct cultural identity. The Nuragic people, who lived in a hierarchical society, were skilled in bronzeworking, creating tools, weapons, and intricate jewelry. Their civilization most likely revolved around agriculture, herding, and trading.

The Nuraghe: Architectural Wonders of the Bronze Age

The nuraghe (plural: nuraghi) is undoubtedly the most characteristic element of the Nuragic culture. The Sardinian countryside is dotted with these impressive megalithic buildings, erected using dry stone construction methods without mortar. Over 7,000 nuraghi have been discovered, with estimates indicating that up to 10,000 may have existed initially.

Nuraghe ranges in size and complexity, from single-tower constructions to huge complexes with several towers, courtyards, and defensive walls. The most elaborate nuraghi have numerous levels connected by internal stairs constructed into the thick stone walls. The function of these nuraghi remains a source of debate. Some think they functioned as fortified towns, providing security against raids and invaders. Others believe they may have had religious or symbolic significance.

Exploring Nuragic Sites: A Journey Through Time.

Sardinia is an open-air museum dedicated to Nuragic heritage. Several archeological sites provide insights into the life and culture of this ancient society. Here are some noteworthy examples:

Su Nuraxi di Barumini: This UNESCO World Heritage Site is the most comprehensive nuragic complex identified. Su Nuraxi, a center tower encircled by a community of houses and defensive fortifications, provides an intriguing peek into Nuragic life.

Su Nuraxi di Barumini, Sardinia.

Nuraghe Losa: This nuragic complex, near Abbasanta, consists of a central tower and surrounding village remnants. The site also has remains of subsequent Punic and Roman colonies, demonstrating the island's complex history.

Nuraghe Losa, Sardinia.

The vast Anghelu Ruju necropolis near Alghero has a collection of Domus de Janas ("houses of the fairies"). These remarkable rock-cut tombs, dating back to the Neolithic era and reused by the Nuragic people, provide information about their burial habits and beliefs.

Necropolis at Anghelu Ruju, Sardinia.

A legacy that endures

The Nuragic culture is still a mystery, with many questions unsolved. Nonetheless, their spectacular design and lasting impact continue to captivate the imagination. Visitors to Sardinia may better understand this distinct culture by visiting archeological sites and learning more about their history.

6.2 Phoenician and Roman influences

Sardinia's fascinating tale goes well beyond the mysterious Nuragic culture. Following the Nuragic period, the island saw the introduction of different civilizations, each with its particular impact on the environment and society. Two significant influences stand out: the Phoenicians and the Romans.

The Phoenicians: Masters of the Sea

Around the eighth century BC, the Phoenicians, expert seafarers and merchants from the eastern Mediterranean, landed on Sardinia's coasts. Initially enticed by the island's rich copper and silver resources, they erected trade stations along the coast, forming communities such as Tharros, Bithia, and Sulci.

Trade, Transformation:

The Phoenicians' involvement in Sardinia was not only for resource exploitation. They brought new technology, agricultural methods, and, most crucially, a thriving trading network that linked Sardinia to the rest of the Mediterranean world. This infusion of trade items and ideas impacted the Nuragic people, causing a progressive cultural transition. Nuragic communities near Phoenician ports grew increasingly elaborate, indicating an expanding elite class and a more centralized social system.

Traces of Phoenician Influence:

While Phoenician constructions have not survived to the same degree as Nuragic nuraghe, their presence may still be felt in Sardinia. Archaeological digs have revealed Phoenician items such as pottery, jewelry, and religious goods. Topheths, holy locations used for child sacrifice, are another evidence of the Phoenician presence on the island.

Phoenician Tophet in Sardinia.

The Romans' Conquest and Legacy

By the third century BC, the Roman Republic had set its eyes on Sardinia. After a lengthy and violent war with the Carthaginians, the Romans took possession of the island in 238 BC. Roman dominance heralded a new period of growth and incorporation within the larger Roman Empire.

Romanization and Infrastructure:

The Romans altered Sardinia, founding new settlements such as Turris Libissonis (modern-day Porto Torres) and encouraging the growth of agriculture and mining. They constructed a vast network of roads, bridges, and aqueducts to link various island sections and facilitate commerce. Roman culture and politics also influenced the architectural styles of multiple cities, with theaters, forums, and temples reflecting this.

Roman remains near Nora, Sardinia.

A Lasting Impact:

The Roman presence in Sardinia left an indelible mark on the island's language, legal system, and administrative institutions. Latin became the primary language, and Roman customs and traditions eventually spread throughout Sardinian culture. Even after the Roman Empire fell, Roman law and administration continued to affect the island's growth.

Sardinia: A Tapestry of Culture

Sardinia's rich past is a fascinating patchwork of many civilizations. Each epoch left its imprint on the island, from the Nuragic people who constructed the mysterious nuraghe to the Phoenicians who introduced commerce and new technologies, and lastly, the Romans who brought conquering and long-lasting infrastructure. Visitors may better understand Sardinia's distinct character and cultural diversity by visiting archaeological sites, immersing themselves in local practices, and learning about the island's history.

6.3 Folklore, Traditions and Festivals

Sardinia's unique narrative is not just engraved in stone or preserved in museums. It lives on via the complex tapestry of folklore, customs, and festivals still enjoyed over the island. From ancient rites to vibrant processions, these demonstrations of cultural identity reveal Sardinia's heart and soul.

Folklore: Weaving Stories from the Past

Sardinian folklore is a rich collection of myths, tales, and stories handed down through centuries. These stories often contain mythological creatures such as "Janas" (fairies) who live in old rock-cut tombs, or "Mamuthones," masked individuals who represent pagan ceremonies. Folk ballads, known as "Canti a Tenore," performed in a distinctive polyphonic manner, weave tales of love, Loss and the island's rich heritage.

Traditions: A Living Heritage.

Traditional crafts continue to flourish in Sardinia. Witness expert artists weaving elaborate reed baskets, making stunning filigree jewelry, and producing vibrant carpets using old methods. Sardinian cuisine, a delectable fusion of local products and culinary influences, is a tradition in and of itself. Enjoy dishes like "culurgiones" (ravioli filled with ricotta cheese and potato), "porceddu" (roasted suckling pig), and "seadas" (fried pastries filled with ricotta cheese and sprinkled with honey).

Festivals are celebrations of life and culture.

Sardinia's calendar is packed with exciting festivities all year. During Carnival festivities, listen to pounding drums and rhythmic chanting as elaborately masked characters such as the "Mamuthones" of Mamoiada and the "Boes and Merdules" of Ottana march through the streets. Witness the equestrian abilities displayed during the "Sartiglia" jousting contest in Oristano, or take in the melancholy grandeur of religious processions during Holy Week festivities.

Here are some of Sardinia's most compelling festivals:

Carnevale: Carnival is celebrated across Sardinia, with variations in each town. It contains extravagant masks, amusing costumes, and vibrant parades. Witness the sight of the "Mamuthones" in Mamoiada or the "Boes and Merdules" in Ottawa, in which masked characters pursue and tease audiences.

Sardinian Carnevale Festival

Settimana Santa (Holy Week) brings religious processions and rituals to life. Witness the solemn grandeur of the Good Friday procession and the joyful joys of Easter Sunday.

Cantine Aperte (Open Cellars): This event, held throughout the spring and summer, enables tourists to explore vineyards, sip local wines, and enjoy Sardinian hospitality.

Sardinian Cantine Aperte Festival.

Nuoro comes alive during the Sagra del Redentore (Festival of the Redeemer), which takes place in late

August and features a colorful parade of costumed individuals and traditional music.

A Journey Beyond the Tourist Trail.

Folklore, customs, and festivals provide a unique glimpse into Sardinia's character. Visitors may obtain a better knowledge of the island's culture and spirit by participating in these festivals, sampling traditional food, and hearing folk stories. So, explore beyond the beaches and historical landmarks, enjoy the rich customs, and be charmed by Sardinia's authentic soul.

Chapter 7: A Taste of Sardinia.

7.1 Sardinian Cuisine: Local Specialties and Must-Try Recipes

Sardinia is more than a visual feast; it's a delectable culinary experience. The island's food has a rich history and distinct tastes, shaped by generations of farmers, shepherds, and fishermen who have perfected using fresh, local ingredients. Prepare to go on a gastronomic trip with these local delicacies and must-try foods that will leave you wanting more:

Fresh from the Sea: Sardinia's coastline is brimming with seafood, and you'd be foolish not to indulge. Enjoy the finest fish, grilled or baked with herbs and olive oil. Dive into a cup of "Zuppa Gallurese" (Gallura Soup), a substantial stew full of seafood tastes and bits of stale bread. For a flavor of local culture, try "Burrida," a fish stew with tomato and saffron sauce.

Sardinian Zuppa Gallurese

Pasta Perfection: Sardinia has a beautiful selection of pasta dishes, each with its distinct touch. Savor "Malloreddus" are little gnocchi-like dumplings often served with sausage ragù. Twirl your fork around a dish of "culurgiones," Sardinian ravioli packed with ricotta cheese and potato and served with a simple tomato sauce. For a vegetarian alternative, consider "Fregola," a small, toasted semolina pasta served in a delicious broth with clams or vegetables.

Sardinian malloreddus

A Taste of the Land: The interior of Sardinia is covered in undulating hills and lush plains that yield a bountiful harvest. Sink your teeth into a piece of "Pane Carasau," a thin, crunchy flatbread that pairs well with olive oil and local cheeses like Pecorino Sardo. Try "Pecorino al Cannonau," which consists of slices of Pecorino cheese soaked in Sardinian Cannonau wine for a delicious taste explosion. Try "Fave," a creamy broad bean purée topped with chopped veggies and olive oil for a vegetarian treat.

Sweet Endings: A dinner is only complete with a touch of sweetness. Enjoy "Seadas," a Sardinian delicacy from deep-fried pastry filled with ricotta cheese and sprinkled with honey. Choose "Casatella," a fresh cheese pie with a citrus filling, for a lighter alternative. To sample local flavors, try "Sardinians," ring-shaped biscuits scented with anise and lemon.

Sardinian cookies.

Liquid Delights: Sardinia has a vibrant wine scene. Raise a glass of Cannonau, a full-bodied red wine from the island. Consider Vermentino, a crisp white wine that pairs well with fish for a lighter choice. Try Mirto, a distinctive Sardinian liqueur derived from myrtle berries, for a refreshing after-dinner drink.

A culinary journey for everyone.

Sardinian cuisine has something for everyone, from fresh seafood meals to robust pasta, savory cheeses, and delectable desserts. For an authentic gastronomic experience while exploring the island, look for local trattorias and family-run osterias rather than tourist eateries. Accept the chance to speak with local chefs and food producers, learn about traditional recipes handed down through generations, and appreciate the authentic flavor of Sardinia. Good appetite!

7.2 Wine regions and Sardinian wines

Sardinia's sun-drenched vineyards and rich history have produced a distinctive wine landscape. As you tour this enchanting island, you will pass through its diverse wine regions, each with its own grape varietals and unique bottles ready to be uncorked.

Cannonau Country: The Heart of Red Wines - Travel to the heart of Sardinia, especially the provinces of Nuoro and Ogliastra, and you will find yourself in Cannonau country. Sardinia's hallmark wine is a robust red produced from the Cannonau vine (also known as Grenache). Take a sip and enjoy its full-bodied flavor, which frequently includes flavors of dark fruit, spice, and a hint of earthiness. For an authentic Sardinian experience, serve Cannonau with grilled meats, robust pasta dishes, or a classic platter of Pecorino Sardo cheese.

Vermentino's Playground: The North and West Shores—Visit the cool, breezy vineyards along Sardinia's northern and western shores, where the Vermentino grape flourishes. This white wine is distinguished by its crisp acidity, refreshing minerality, and subtle floral and citrus notes. Take a drink and appreciate its versatility: Vermentino works well with seafood, light pasta, or as an aperitif on a warm Sardinian evening.

Exploring the Unique: Native Grapes and Blends—Sardinia is more than simply Cannonau and Vermentino. Explore wines created from Indigenous grape varieties rarely seen on the market. Explore Gallura's rich, full-bodied Nieddu reds or Cagliari's fascinating Nasco whites. The island also has fascinating blends, in which winemakers mix foreign grapes such as Cabernet Sauvignon with Indigenous varietals to produce new and nuanced wines. Be bold and ask your waitress or local wine store owner for tips on these hidden treasures.

Visit a vineyard to learn about the winemaking process and immerse yourself in the world of Sardinian wine. Many vineyards provide tours and tastings, which enable you to see the winemaking process firsthand. Stroll around the vineyards to learn about the grape varieties planted on the estate and the ancient and contemporary procedures used to produce these excellent wines. Most importantly, conclude your tour with a tasting session to experience the distinct flavors created by each vineyard and learn about the devotion that goes into each bottle.

Beyond the Bottle: Wine Festivals and Events - Sardinia celebrates its wine culture annually. Participate in a lively "Cantine Aperte" (Open Cellars) event, where wineries welcome visitors for tastings, local food pairings, and live music. Immerse yourself in the joyous atmosphere of a local wine festival, where you may taste a diverse range of wines from various areas and producers. These events provide an excellent chance to learn about Sardinian wines, meet local winemakers, and find new favorites.

Sardinia's wine scene is a thrilling adventure waiting to be discovered. From the timeless elegance of Cannonau to the refreshing appeal of Vermentino and the captivating island's broad assortment of indigenous grapes and mixes caters to every taste. So lift a glass, appreciate the aromas, and allow Sardinia's wines to transport you on an incredible journey.

7.3 Restaurants and Nightlife

Sardinia is more than simply beautiful beaches and fascinating history; it's also a refuge for informal and gourmet eating and exciting nightlife. As you tour the island, prepare to delight your taste senses and dance the night away.

A Culinary Journey: Discovering Sardinian Flavors.

Trattorias & Family-run Osterias:

For a natural flavor of Sardinia, visit a local trattoria or family-run osteria. These humble eateries represent the heart and spirit of Sardinian food. In intimate settings, savor handmade pasta delicacies such as "Malloreddus" (little gnocchi-like dumplings) and "Culurgiones" (ravioli stuffed with ricotta and potato). Enjoy fresh seafood meals or slow-cooked meats made using generations-old traditions. Here are a few tips to help you get started:

- **La Cucina di Mamma Teresa (Alghero):** This beautiful trattoria in Alghero has a welcoming environment and serves exquisite Sardinian dishes such as suckling pig and seafood spaghetti.

- **Il Pescatore (Cagliari):** Located in the heart of Cagliari's ancient city, Il Pescatore is a seafood lover's paradise. Enjoy fresh seafood served, allowing the sea flavors to come through.

- **Trattoria da Romano (San Pantaleo):** This restaurant provides an enjoyable alfresco-eating experience in the lovely town of San Pantaleo. Enjoy traditional Sardinian meals and local wines for an unforgettable evening.

Fine Dining with a Sardinian Twist: If you want a more upmarket culinary experience, Sardinia has several excellent fine dining places. These restaurants highlight the island's fresh, local foods via creative methods and attractive displays. Prepare to savor inventive interpretations of traditional Sardinian foods and an extensive wine selection. There are a few choices to consider:

- **La Sponda (Cala Mariolu):** Perched on a cliff overlooking the gorgeous Cala Mariolu beach, La Sponda serves fantastic views and a cuisine of fresh seafood and Sardinian delicacies with a contemporary touch.

- **Dal Corsaro (Cagliari):** Located in Cagliari's old Castello neighborhood, Dal Corsaro has an exquisite setting and a menu highlighting the finest Sardinian cuisine with a Mediterranean flair.

- **Aria (Porto Cervo):** For an opulent dining experience, visit Aria in Porto Cervo. This Michelin-starred restaurant has fantastic views of the Costa Smeralda and serves inventive meals made with the best Sardinian ingredients.

Nightlife Highlights: From Chic Cocktail Bars to Lively Discos.

Sardinia's nightlife scene caters to every taste. As the sun goes down, the island turns into a thriving center of activity:

- **Chic Cocktail Bars:** Begin your evening with a classy drink from a trendy cocktail bar. Expert mixologists create unique cocktails using local ingredients and quality spirits. Immerse yourself in the fashionable environment of these restaurants, ideal for pre-dinner cocktails or a laid-back evening out. Here are some suggestions:

- **The Old Fashion (Cagliari):** This tiny bar in Cagliari serves an outstanding assortment of whiskeys and traditional cocktails made with meticulous attention to detail.

- **The Wine Bar (Porto Cervo):** Located in the heart of the beautiful Costa Smeralda, The Wine Bar serves an extensive wine selection, unique drinks, and an attractive setting.

- **Lively Discos and Beach Clubs:** If you want to dance the night away, visit one of Sardinia's many discos or beach clubs. These places are bustling with throbbing music, lively people, and a celebratory atmosphere. Prepare to dance beneath the stars and explore Sardinia's bustling nightlife scene. Some prominent alternatives are:

- **Ritual Club (Cagliari):** This well-known disco in Cagliari draws audiences with its worldwide DJs, live music events, and upbeat ambiance.

- **Phi Beach (Baja Sardinia):** This open-air beach club in Baja Sardinia has breathtaking sunset views, world-class DJs, and a secluded party atmosphere. Prepare to dress to impress for this beautiful event.

Part 4: Practical Information.

Chapter 8: Accommodation Options in Sardinia.

8.1 Luxury Hotels and Resorts.

Sardinia is more than just a gorgeous island; it's a playground for the wealthy, with various opulent resorts and hotels that redefine luxury, exclusivity, and service. Prepare to be pampered as you discover these havens, each with breathtaking sites, excellent facilities, and activities that will take your breath away.

The epitome of beachside bliss:

Forte Village Resort (Santa Margherita di Pula): Experience incomparable luxury at Forte Village Resort, a massive resort on Sardinia's southern coast. This resort has a range of hotels to meet your needs, including the family-friendly Hotel Pineta and the ultra-exclusive Hotel Il Castello. Imagine gorgeous beaches, championship golf courses, world-class spas, Michelin-starred restaurants, and a private marina all at your fingertips. During peak season, overnight costs may vary from €1,000 to €3,000, depending on the hotel and room type.

Forte Village Resort in Sardinia

Romazzino, A Belmond Hotel (Costa Smeralda): Located on the beautiful Costa Smeralda, Romazzino, a Belmond Hotel exudes elegance and refinement. Imagine luxury villas with infinity pools overlooking the turquoise waves, a world-class spa that provides revitalizing treatments, and various gourmet restaurants serving fine Italian and international cuisine. Prepare for an extraordinary adventure, with nightly prices beginning at €2,000 and increasing depending on the season and villa selected.

7Pines Resort Sardinia (Baja Sardinia): Experience a modern twist on luxury at 7Pines Resort Sardinia. This stylish resort sits on a clifftop overlooking Cala Marina Bay. Relax in sleek, minimalist suites with private patios, enjoy relaxing treatments at the COMO Shambhala spa, and dine at the resort's restaurants, which serve superb meals made with fresh, local ingredients. During peak season, nightly prices are generally between €1,500 and €2,500.

7 Pines Resort Sardinia

Historic Charm and Modern Luxuries:

Baglioni Resort Sardinia (Cala del Mortorio): Step back in time while enjoying contemporary amenities at Baglioni Resort Sardinia. This magnificent refuge, housed in a former 16th-century watchtower, offers a one-of-a-kind combination of history and modern design. Relax in exquisite accommodations with stunning sea views, taste great Italian food at the panoramic terrace restaurant, and bask in the sun beside the resort's infinity pool. During the peak season, nightly costs might vary between €1,200 and €2,000.

Baglioni Resort Sardinia

Hotel Cala di Volpe, a Luxury Collection Hotel (Costa Smeralda), offers timeless elegance. For decades, this legendary resort, part of Marriott's Luxury Collection, has served as a retreat for celebrities and discriminating guests. Imagine luxuriating in ample accommodations with private balconies overlooking Cala di Volpe Bay, receiving revitalizing treatments at the famous spa, and eating at the resort's fine-dining restaurants. Prepare for nightly costs to start at €1,800 and rise depending on the season and room type.

Longevity Suite Hotel (Costa Rei): Sardinia's East Coast hotel offers a wellness-focused luxury experience. This unique resort blends individualized wellness programs, elegant rooms, and stunning seaside views. Modern workout facilities, a world-class spa with cutting-edge treatments, and an emphasis on healthy, tasty food are all on the agenda. Nightly charges often vary between €1,000 and €1,500.

These are just a few of the excellent luxury resorts and hotels Sardinia has on offer. On this exquisite island, you may indulge, relax, and make beautiful memories in various settings, from significant coastal havens to quaint historic retreats. Remember that these are just starting points; costs may vary based on the season, room availability, and special offers. Research and evaluate choices to discover the best match for your preferences and budget.

8.2 Boutique Hotels and Charming Bed & Breakfasts

Sardinia's hospitality scene goes far beyond the great resorts. For a more private and customized experience, try staying in a lovely boutique hotel or a comfortable bed and breakfast. These hidden jewels provide distinct atmospheres, excellent service, and the opportunity to immerse yourself in the island's character:

Boutique Hideaways: Chic Design and Personal Attention

Locanda La Frescura (Alghero): Located in the heart of Alghero's old city, Locanda La Frescura is a peaceful refuge. This magnificently renovated 19th-century building has only a few distinctively designed rooms, each bursting with Sardinian charm and contemporary comforts. On the rooftop patio, you may have a bespoke breakfast made with local ingredients while admiring the views of the town and port. Nightly costs often vary between €250 and €400.

CBoutique Hotel (Cagliari): For a modern boutique experience in Cagliari, go no further than the CBoutique Hotel. This beautiful hotel is housed in a refurbished 16th-century edifice that perfectly blends historic charm and contemporary design. Unwind in stylish rooms with exposed stone walls and designer furniture. The hotel's rooftop terrace has magnificent city views and is ideal for an evening aperitif. Expect overnight costs to vary between €300 and €500.

Su Gologone Boutique Hotel (Baunei): Escape to Sardinia's spectacular east coast and stay at Su Gologone. This tiny cottage tucked amid olive orchards provides a tranquil setting and stunning mountain views. Relax in nicely designed rooms with private balconies, dine on excellent Sardinian cuisine in the hotel's famous restaurant, and explore the surrounding beaches and coves. During peak season, nightly prices average between €400 and €600.

Charming bed and breakfasts: Sardinian hospitality at its finest.

Il Giardino delle Meraviglie (Castelsardo): Enjoy genuine Sardinian hospitality at Il Giardino delle Meraviglie, a delightful bed and breakfast in the scenic town of Castelsardo. This carefully renovated stone home has pleasant rooms furnished with traditional Sardinian fabrics. Enjoy a great prepared breakfast with local favorites on the flower-filled terrace. Immerse yourself in the local environment and see the neighboring beaches and Doria Castle. Nightly costs usually vary between €150 and €250.

Relais Albergo San Giovanni (Bosa): For a romantic retreat, visit Relais Albergo San Giovanni in the lovely village of Bosa. This ancient tower, formerly a 14th-century convent, contains exquisite rooms with exposed stone walls and traditional furniture. Relax in the tranquil courtyard garden, have excellent breakfasts made with locally sourced food, and explore the town's vibrant streets and historic bridge. Nightly charges often vary between €200 and €300.

Can Curreu (Orgosolo): If you want a genuine Sardinian experience, Can Curreu in Orgosolo may be the place to go. This old stone farmhouse has become a comfortable bed and breakfast, providing a look into country life. The kind proprietors will welcome you with open arms and share their enthusiasm for the island. Enjoy handmade breakfasts cooked with local ingredients and explore the nearby Supramonte mountains, famed for their hiking paths and stunning landscapes. Nightly costs generally vary between €100 and €180.

These are just a handful of the numerous beautiful boutique hotels and bed and breakfasts that dot the Sardinian countryside. Whether you want a stylish urban getaway, a romantic hideaway, or a taste of traditional

Sardinian hospitality, a hidden treasure is waiting to be found. Remember that costs vary according to the season and availability, so do your homework and book your stay ahead of time, particularly during the high season.

8.3 Self-catering Apartments and Villas.

Sardinia is more than simply magnificent hotels with beautiful beds and breakfasts. Staying in a self-catering apartment or villa provides a more autonomous and flexible holiday experience. Consider having your private room to unwind, prepare meals quickly, and explore the island at your leisure. Here's a taste of the varied possibilities Sardinia provides:

Beachfront Bliss: Apartments with Amazing Sea Views

Cala Marina Luxury Apartments (Cala Marina): At Cala Marina Luxury Apartments, you may live your dream of waking up to stunning ocean views. These new apartments, situated only steps from the beach in Cala Marina on the east coast, provide an ideal balance of comfort and design. Prepare meals in your fully equipped kitchen, relax on your balcony with breathtaking sea views, and have the flexibility to create your Sardinian beach vacation. Weekly fees are expected to vary between €1,500 and €2,500, depending on the apartment size and season.

Le Dune Beach Apartments (Costa Rei): For a family-friendly choice on the south coast, look into Le Dune Beach Apartments in Costa Rei. These large flats within walking distance of the beach provide an ideal base for exploring the region. Cook meals together in the fully equipped kitchen, relax on the furnished balcony, and enjoy the on-site swimming pool, which is ideal for cooling down after a day at the beach. Weekly fees usually vary between €800 and €1,200, depending on the size of the flat and the season.

Staying at Al Colle Apartments in Stintino, a picturesque coastal town famed for its clean beaches, immerses yourself in the area's beauty. These attractively designed apartments have fantastic views of the turquoise waves, and La Pelosa beach is frequently voted one of Italy's most beautiful. Prepare fresh seafood dinners in your kitchen, relax on your balcony, and explore the surrounding beaches and coves at your leisure. Weekly costs usually vary between €1,000 and €1,800, depending on the flat size and season.

Rustic Charm Villas Nestled in the Sardinian Countryside

Son Matias Country House in Alghero offers a peaceful retreat in the Sardinian countryside. This wonderfully renovated stone farmhouse has a private home with a swimming pool, surrounded by olive orchards and vineyards. Imagine creating meals in the traditional kitchen with fresh local products, sitting by the pool with stunning views, and enjoying the tranquility of the rural area. Weekly fees typically run between €1,200 and €2,000, depending on the season.

Villa Sa Conca (Cala Gonone): For an exciting getaway on the east coast, choose Villa Sa Conca in Cala Gonone. This beautiful cottage, set among olive orchards and with spectacular sea views, is an excellent base for exploring the Baunei coastline's adjacent beaches, caves, and hiking paths. Prepare beautiful dinners on the BBQ with local products, relax in the private pool, and take in the natural surroundings. Weekly fees vary between €800 and €1,500, depending on the season.

Staying at Mozia Villa in Teulada allows you to immerse yourself in Sardinian history and culture. This renovated 19th-century farmhouse has a distinct combination of classic architecture and contemporary comforts. The property has a private swimming pool and a large yard ideal for al fresco eating. It is conveniently located near historical attractions and attractive towns to visit. Weekly fees vary between €1,000 and €1,800, depending on the season.

These are just a handful of Sardinia's numerous self-catering apartments and villas. From coastal havens to beautiful rural getaways, you'll discover a property that meets your needs and budget. Remember that rates vary based on the season, property size, and available facilities. Study and reserve your accommodations in advance, particularly during the high season.

8.4 Camping and glamping sites

Sardinia is more than magnificent resorts and attractive villages; it's also a paradise for outdoor enthusiasts and environment lovers. Immerse yourself in the island's natural splendor by going camping or glamping. Imagine waking up to nature's noises, spending your days discovering secret coves, and stargazing beneath a beautiful night sky. Here's a taste of the varied possibilities Sardinia provides:

Camping under the stars: Traditional campsites with Sardinian charm.

Camping La Pineta (Sos Alinos): Nestled amid pine trees on the east coast of Sos Alinos, Camping La Pineta provides a traditional camping experience. Pitch your tent or rent a cottage in the thick nature, only feet from a stunning sandy beach. Enjoy the on-site amenities, such as a swimming pool, café, and playground, ideal for families. Nightly fees for a modest campground typically run between €20 and €40, depending on the season.

Camping Isuledda (Santa Teresa Gallura) offers fantastic views. This family-friendly campground has sites for tents and campers as well as mobile homes and bungalows for those who want more luxury. Enjoy immediate access to a magnificent beach, relax in the on-site swimming pool, or visit the adjacent Capo Testa nature reserve, which has stunning granite rock formations. Nightly costs for a simple campground typically run between €25 and €50, depending on the season.

Camping Laguna Blu (Cala Gonone) offers an opportunity to explore the stunning Baunei shoreline on the east coast. This campground has many alternatives, including simple tent sites and mobile homes with individual terraces. Enjoy the on-site restaurant serving excellent Sardinian cuisine, take advantage of the boat cruises from the adjacent harbor to discover secret coves and caves, or trekking in the neighboring mountains. Nightly costs for a modest campground typically run between €15 and €35, depending on the season.

Glamping in Style: Luxury Camping Experiences

Experience the glamping trend at Chitzen Glamping in San Teodoro. Consider sleeping in a roomy, beautiful safari tent with comfy mattresses, a private toilet, and a furnished deck. Enjoy the on-site swimming pool, relax in the shared lounge area, and discover the local beaches and picturesque town of San Teodoro. Nightly fees vary between €150 and €300, depending on the season and tent type.

Arbatax Park Camping Resort (Arbatax) offers a magnificent glamping experience with various facilities on the east coast. This resort provides a variety of glamping choices, including romantic wood cabins and huge glamping tents with private pools. Enjoy the on-site restaurants, swimming pools, water park, and entertainment choices, which are ideal for families and groups of friends. Nightly costs usually vary from €200 to €500, depending on the season and glamping accommodation selected.

Telis Experience (Cala Brandinchi) offers a one-of-a-kind glamping experience near Cala Brandinchi, often known as "Little Tahiti" because of its turquoise seas and white sand beach. Imagine living in a luxury yurt, a traditional Mongolian housing outfitted with all home amenities, just feet from the beautiful beach. Visit the on-site wellness center, which offers yoga classes and massages, or explore the neighboring coves and hiking trails. Nightly costs usually vary between €250 and €400, depending on the season and yurt style.

These are just a handful of the numerous camping and glamping sites spread over Sardinia. Whether you want a conventional back-to-nature experience or a lavish glamping retreat with all the conveniences, you'll be able to find an option that meets your needs and budget. Remember that rates vary based on the season, location, and kind of lodging available. Investigate and reserve your space in advance, particularly during high season.

Chapter 9: Maintaining Connection and Communication

9.1 Mobile Phone Coverage and Internet Access

Sardinia typically offers adequate mobile phone service; nonetheless, there are specific considerations to consider.

- **Coverage:** Sardinia is covered by all of Italy's leading mobile network carriers (TIM, Vodafone, and Windtre). This implies that you should be able to make calls and utilize data in most towns, cities, and on major roads.

- **Rural locations:** Remote and hilly locations, like many others, might have patchy or non-existent mobile phone service. If you want to go off the usual route, get any maps or information you need beforehand.

- **Network Choice:** Vodafone is widely regarded as having the finest overall coverage in Italy, including rural regions. However, TIM and Windtre both provide adequate coverage around the island.

- **3G vs. 4G/5G:** While 4G and even 5G coverage are becoming more ubiquitous in Sardinia, particularly in densely populated regions, 3G remains more prevalent. This implies that you may experience slower internet connections in certain areas.

Here are some sites that can help you assess mobile phone coverage in Sardinia before your trip.

- **Mobile Network Operator Websites:** Each primary provider's website (TIM, Vodafone, Windtre) has a coverage map. You may look for particular areas in Sardinia to discover how strong the signal is for each network.

- **Travel Forums and Reviews:** Many travel forums and review websites discuss mobile phone coverage in Sardinia. Reading these might provide you with insights into other travelers' experiences.

Internet Access:

- **Mobile Data:** If you have a solid mobile phone connection, you may use your phone's data plan to access the internet in Sardinia. Check with your cell operator regarding roaming costs, particularly if you're going from outside of Europe.

- **Wi-Fi** is available in hotels, restaurants, cafés, and public locations around Sardinia. The quality and speed of Wi-Fi may vary depending on the area.

Tips to Stay Connected in Sardinia:

- Consider buying a prepaid SIM card from a local cell provider in Sardinia. This is more cost-effective than using your phone's roaming plan, particularly if you intend to use a lot of data.
- **Download Offline Maps and Material:** Before you go, download maps and any other material you need (such as guidebooks or restaurant reviews). This allows you to access the information even if you do not have an internet connection.
- Let People Know Your Travel Plans: If you're worried about losing contact in remote places, tell your friends and family about your trip and when you intend to return to an area with solid mobile phone service.

9.2 Staying Safe: Emergency Numbers and Services.

Sardinia is typically a safe destination, but you should always be prepared in case of an emergency. Here are the most important numbers and services to remember throughout your vacation.

Emergency Numbers:

- **Emergency Services:** 112 - This is the one emergency number for all emergency services in Italy, including police, ambulances, and fire departments. You may call this number free from any phone, even without a SIM card.

- **The Carabinieri (National Gendarmerie)** may be reached at 112 (from a mobile phone) or 113 (from a landline). They are Italy's national police force, in charge of law enforcement and public safety.

- **The Polizia di Stato (State Police)** may be reached at 112 (from a mobile phone) or 113 (from a landline). They conduct criminal investigations and traffic management.

- **Ambulance:** 118 - Call this number if you need an ambulance in an emergency.

Additional Important Numbers:

- **Fire Department:** 115 - Call this number during a fire.
- Coast Guard: 1530 - Contact the Coast Guard if you have an emergency at sea or need help with maritime matters.

- **Traffic Police:** You may get the phone number for the local traffic police station by searching online or inquiring at your hotel or lodging.

Safety Tips:

- **Be alert of your surroundings:** This basic safety guideline applies anywhere you go. Pay care to your valuables, particularly in busy places.

- **Carry a copy of your passport:** It's always a good idea to have a duplicate on hand in case you lose the original.

- **Learn some fundamental Italian phrases:** Knowing a few simple Italian words might be helpful in an emergency.

- **Buy travel insurance:** Travel insurance may provide financial protection for medical problems, travel cancellations, or misplaced baggage.

Medical Service:

- Pharmacies in Sardinia are readily identified by their green cross signs. Many pharmacies remain open late or provide 24-hour service.

- **Hospitals:** Various hospitals are spread around Sardinia. Ask your hotel or lodging about the closest hospital or clinic if you need medical treatment.

Additional resources:

Consider downloading the "Where are You" app, which connects to Italy's emergency services. This software might be helpful if you don't speak Italian or need to locate your position for emergency personnel.

By familiarizing yourself with these emergency numbers and services, you can ensure a safe and pleasurable holiday in Sardinia.

Appendix
A1: Maps of Sardinia

A2. Glossary of Sardinian Terms

While Sardinian is not a commonly spoken language outside of the island, here is some helpful terminology you may come across during your trip:

Greetings and Common Phrases:

- Good day (boon-jor-no). Good morning/Hello (formal).
- Hello (chow): Hello/goodbye (informal)
- Thanks (gra-tsee-eh): Thank you!
- Prego (pronounced: pre-go): You are welcome. Please, Scusi (pronounced scu-see). Excuse me.
- Si (See): Yes
- No (no): No
- My name is Mee Kia-mo. Hi, my name is
- Parla inglese: Do you speak English?
- Non capisco (ka-pees-co): I need help comprehending

Food and Drinks.

- Pane (pah-neh): Bread is a staple in Sardinia.
- Formaggio (pronounced for-mah-jo): Cheese
- Vino (Vee-No): Wine - Sardinia has a rich winemaking heritage.
- Birra (pronounced "beer-ra"): Acqua (pronounced "ah-kwa") refers to beer. Water: Frutta (froo-ta) Fruit

- Pesce (pronounced pesh-eh): Fish Carne (pronounced "car-neh"): Ristorante, pronounced "ree-staw-rahn-teh," refers to meat. Restaurant

Bar (Bar): Bar Locations and Directions:

- Spiaggia (beach),
- Mare (sea),
- Montagna (mountain),
- Città (city),
- Paese (town/village), and
- Negozio (nego-tsee-o). Shop,
- Piazza (square),
- Museo (museum), and
- Chiesa (chieh-za).
- Synonyms for the church include "dove" (where), "come" (how), and "sinistra" (see). Left: Destra (des-tra) Right:

Numbers (1–10)

- Uno (OO-NO)
- Due (doo-eh).
- Tre (treh).
- Quadro (kilowatts)
- Cinque (Chink-Veh)
- Say (sei)
- Sette (set-the
- Otto (Ot-to)
- Nove (pronounced no-veh).
- Dieci (dee-eh-chi)

Additional Useful Words:

- Thank you very much (gra-tsee-eh mee-leh). Thank you very much.
- Arrivederci (pronounced ar-ree-veh-der-chi): Hello (formal)
- Buona sera (boo-nah seh-rah). Good evening.
- Per favore (per fah-voh-reh). Please aiuto (ah-oo-to): Help
- How much does it cost? How much does it cost?
- Speak a little Italian. I speak a little Italian.

This is just a tiny sample of Sardinian words. Remember that Italian is commonly spoken in Sardinia. Therefore, many of the above words may also be used in Italian.

Printed in Great Britain
by Amazon